The Caregiver's Choice

The Caregiver's Choice

Find Strength and Serenity by Changing Your Mind

Elaine Long

iUniverse, Inc.
New York   Bloomington   Shanghai

The Caregiver's Choice
Find Strength and Serenity by Changing Your Mind

iUniverse books may be ordered through booksellers or by contacting:

iUniverse
1663 Liberty Drive
Bloomington, IN 47403
www.iuniverse.com
1-800-Authors (1-800-288-4677)

Because of the dynamic nature of the Internet, any Web addresses or links contained in this book may have changed since publication and may no longer be valid.

The information, ideas, and suggestions in this book are not intended as a substitute for professional advice. Before following any suggestions contained in this book, you should consult your personal physician or mental health professional. Neither the author nor the publisher shall be liable or responsible for any loss or damage allegedly arising as a consequence of your use or application of any information or suggestions in this book.

ISBN: 978-0-595-49018-9 (pbk)
ISBN: 978-0-595-49363-0 (cloth)
ISBN: 978-0-595-60932-1 (ebk)

Printed in the United States of America

For caregivers everywhere

In memory of

Arthur W. Long: 7-31-1923 to 1-31-2003
Evelyn Mullenax: 9-12-1909 to 4-13-2007

A note to the reader

I began this book in 1999 and often loaned the rough manuscript to people who seemed to need the information in it. The cover quotes are from people who have used the book in their own caregiving experience. After my husband's death in 2003, I amended the text to mention his death. I finished the book in early 2007. My mother died in April of that year, but I have not changed the text to include her death. I provide this information here to encourage caregivers who have projects of their own to keep working on them even while they are caregiving. It can be done.

Acknowledgments

James Crutchfield always provides intelligent counsel and caring friendship. Without him, this book would never have reached publication. Thanks, Jim.

I am grateful to my siblings Doris Osborne, Mary Chase, and John Mullenax for growing along with me during the long years of our mother's dementia.

Thank you also to all my mother's nieces, nephews, grandchildren, and friends who visited and continued to love and support her even when she no longer recognized them.

I am grateful to Jeanne Williams, Kathleen O'Neal Gear, Lisa Forsyth, Stuart Hachmann, Cheryl Metz, Maria Martin, Don Vincent, Teclia Cunningham, Haven Stillwater, Matthew Burkley, M.D., and many more people for their encouraging words about the book.

Without the help of my daughter, Mary K. Long, and my sister-in-law Evelyn Bashor, I could not have been a double caregiver during the last months of my husband's life. My thanks and blessings.

Contents

Preface

Having worked with Elaine caring for her mother, I witnessed first hand how her approach to the caregiver role benefitted not only her mother but also the staff and fellow residents where her mother resided until her death. Most importantly, Elaine changed my own attitude and approach to patients with dementia. Her insight and clarity, born of experience, make this book an invaluable resource for anyone caught in this profoundly difficult role.

—Matthew D. Burkley, M.D.

Foreword

To those who care *and give care …*

At some time, many of us become caregivers, not as parents beguiled by a child's growth, not as nurses through temporary illness or injury, but for the rest of a loved one's life, with no respite or hope of improvement. The illuminations in this book are the fruit of Elaine Long's more than fourteen years of caring for her mother as Alzheimer's progressed and her own husband's health failed so that she was trying to meet the needs of two people.

I read this manuscript before and after a trip to stay with my thirty-nine-year-old daughter, for whom I have been guardian, conservator, and part-time caregiver since a brain injury several years ago. Trying to help my once brilliant, beautiful daughter have some kind of life is the hardest ordeal I've faced. *The Caregiver's Choice* has given me comfort, hope, and usable suggestions.

Accepting that it is truly your *choice* to give liberates energy that might otherwise be tied up in resentment. That basic anchor can hold you through many storms. The chapter on releasing relatives will be useful for those who futilely expect help from their families. Finding areas where family members can help even if they are either unable or unwilling to be directly involved with caregiving is Elaine's creative and blame-reducing solution that leaves all concerned feeling better.

Full of practical means to better your loved one's life, the book emphasizes the need to love and care for yourself and to find ways to replenish your physical and emotional reserves. For Elaine, these ways include flying, meditation, playing her guitar, or leisure over gourmet coffee. For a friend of mine, it was prowling vintage clothing shops. For me, it's gardening, hiking, my cats and dogs, and reading. A refreshing note throughout is Elaine's recognition that what works for her may not be the answer for you, but you can find your own ways to let your depleted fountain fill and sparkle.

Free of jargon, full of conviction and nitty-gritty truth, Elaine's book will help any caregiver. This is a handbook to return to in times of special stress. I know that I'll often strengthen myself with the chapters on what might be called the Deadly Sins of the caregiver: grief, anger, and guilt.

I find special comfort and hope in the last chapter, where Elaine says, "I believe that when the outer, material self changes, the inner self is not altered … The whole self seems to be made of a lovely form of light." She found that light in her mother and the other people in that locked Alzheimer's unit, and she shows us how to find it, too.

—Jeanne Williams, caregiver mom, author

Introduction

Our carts bumped together in the Wal Mart aisle. "They didn't make the aisles any wider in their new store, did they?" I said cheerfully as I re-aimed my cart to move past the woman whose cart had swerved and tapped mine.

"No," the woman said, "they didn't. And I don't *need* any more aggravation."

The tight, teeth-gritted tone of the woman's voice was familiar to me, and I paused to really look at her face. Beneath the blond hair, which was a little too long for its own style, above the faded sweatshirt chosen for convenience, not fashion, I saw all the signs I have seen in my own mirror: weary eyes, tight jaw muscles, suppressed fury and desperation in every downward line.

In January 1993, after my mother was diagnosed with Alzheimer's disease and after several other care solutions had been tried unsuccessfully, my husband, Arthur, and I agreed to take my mother into our home and give her twenty-four-hour care. It was a decision I felt I had to make. Arthur agreed out of principle. We knew nothing of the realities of the disease. The physical and emotional stress created by our decision was nearly unbearable for all three of us. My husband spoke of those months as the worst of his entire life.

When our situation became impossible to sustain, when we could not keep my mother safe, when our marriage was at risk, when my health was breaking, when my writing career was at a standstill, I knew I had to make other arrangements for my mother's care. Because my mother refused to cooperate, though unable to make appropriate decisions or to care for herself, I was required to go to court to become her legal guardian. After the sad court hearing, I moved my mother to a nursing home thirty-two miles away from our home in the mountains.

Now, in 2007, my mother continues the slow and torturous downhill slide, some new loss attending each degree of decline. I still travel 128 miles a week to make my twice-weekly visits—unless the phone rings and the familiar voice of the duty nurse asks for me. Then I am called to go sooner and oftener, frequently despite snow or darkness. I never know what I will find when I arrive, except that it will be upsetting or they wouldn't have called me. Such a routine is emotionally exhausting, and until 1996, I carried my fatigue and distress home to my husband, who to the best of his ability tried to help me find a way to ease my burden. Unfortunately, the burden I imposed on *him* may have been too much.

In 1996, my husband had a heart attack. I drove him eight miles to the medical center in the small town nearest us. He was taken from there by ambulance to the hospital and by helicopter to a larger hospital one hundred miles away for surgery. Then he came home to me, and I became a caregiver at both ends of the valley.

But Arthur did not thrive. Several months after the heart attack, he was diagnosed as having diabetes. Our entire lifestyle changed. I learned how to run the blood-pressure monitor and the glucose monitor. Our diet also changed completely, requiring me to learn new methods of cooking and to look desperately for some way to put a little pleasure into his life when he had been forced to give up all the small joys that ease stress and add sparkle to a day.

Despite the changes we had made, eighteen months after the heart attack, my husband went into a frightening decline that the doctors could not understand. He became so weak that he could not rise from a table or get out of his recliner unless I lifted him, a huge and uncertain endeavor, since he weighed seventy pounds more than I did. His leg muscles cramped and he could not ride a mile in a car without stopping to try to walk away the pain. Finally, and only with the help of our local pharmacist, we discovered that he was having severe side effects to a drug prescribed to prevent angina.

After a change of medicine, Arthur recovered some of his strength, but in November of 2002, he was diagnosed with terminal lung cancer. He died in our home on January 31, 2003.

During my husband's bouts with illness, I did not feel that I could neglect my mother. Torn by storms of fear, despair, confusion, resentment, fatigue, sorrow, anger, and self-pity, I was an emotional mess. At one point in 1996, I was asked for a photograph to be used at a writers' seminar in which I was to take part. I was horrified when I saw the photographer's proofs. Usually too busy to do more than run a brush through my hair and smear on a bit of lipstick, I had been aware only subliminally how much of my turmoil showed on my face.

The stark, ugly emptiness of the face in the photographer's proofs was a shock. I realized then that I would have to change to survive. If I could just take a month off, a week away from my duties, a day to myself ... but that was not possible. Like caregivers all over the country, all over the world, despite lawmakers' promises, despite institutions that help, I was faced with the one truth we caregivers know. You can't quit. When you've made the choice to be a caregiver, you keep on keeping on, unless you break.

The blond woman in front of me with her shopping cart was about to break. I abandoned for the moment my need to hurry to the checkout counter, and said to her, "When you're under stress, everything is more aggravating, isn't it?"

That's all it took. Gripping the cart handle until her knuckles were white, the woman poured out a tale of caring for a sister with cancer and of facing increasing responsibility for a mother who was going blind yet refused any solution but that her already burdened daughter take on full care of her. I simply waited and listened, letting the woman talk until she seemed to come back into herself. Then she wiped her eyes and gave me a rueful smile. "I have to go. I'm late. I'm sorry. I didn't mean to dump all that on you." Though embarrassed, she was somewhat less miserable, and when I opened my arms, she came quickly into them, taking and returning a strong hug of understanding.

I have not seen the woman again since that day in 1999, but I think often of her, because I realized two things as she hurried away. First, and with a great quiet joy, I realized *I am no longer desperate.* At that time my mother was losing her teeth and losing weight and lapsing into painful silences when she wasn't careening crazily around the ward grabbing other residents and causing problems. My husband's health had stabilized somewhat, but we still had to be watchful, and I still continued to give care. But caregiving was no longer killing me! The second thing I realized that day in Wal Mart was just how much I care about caregivers.

Judging by all tangible measurements, such as wages, benefits, time off, vacation, recognition, or even acknowledgment of the value of the vast unpaid workforce called caregivers, a caregiver would be justified in feeling that her role was at the lowest end of all the country's charts. (Even professional caregivers are at the low end of those charts.) There are volunteer organizations and support groups (usually made up of other tired, wonderful caregivers) that offer some measure of relief, but even after talking with such groups, I felt the fatigue and despair that lined my face, took the joy from eyes, and left me tired and desolate and empty. What I was forced to realize was that, in order to survive and keep on going, in order to reach a measure of peace, I needed to change something about *me.*

I am not a doctor or a psychiatrist, but I've talked to them, and though some of them seem to care, doctors and psychiatrists don't necessarily understand how a caregiver *feels.* Legislators don't understand how caregiving can wreck a profession and wring the life out of a life, and I am not certain that they care at all. Family members who are not the main caregiver don't know what happens on a daily basis.

It takes serious mental work to move beyond the search for someone, *anyone,* to help you survive as a caregiver. I had been a caregiver for nearly three years before I began doing that work. Soon, I noticed that more caregivers were asking me questions about how I coped so well. And I realized as I looked in the mirror that I no longer resembled the debris thrown up on the beach after a storm and a shipwreck at sea.

What did I do? *I changed my mind.* It was—and is—difficult because many of the attitudes I've rearranged or abandoned are those that society reinforces and approves, often on a hidden level. Some will scoff and say that I'm kidding myself. Others will suggest that I am suppressing my feelings. Since honesty is one of the absolutes in my new attitude, I remain open to the possibility that I need to release suppressed feelings just to keep my mental housecleaning done. That makes sense.

However, I'm not concerned with people who make comments and give advice but *aren't* caregivers and choose never to be. They can't speak truly of me unless they've been where I've been, and will go where I have yet to go. This book is not for them.

This book is for Joanna, who patiently, sweetly feeds her husband of thirty-six years in the nursing home each day, not knowing for sure that he even knows her; for Dick, who cares for his wife at home, never away more than an hour; for Elmer, who shops for adult diapers and pushes a wheelchair, quietly and steadily faithful; for Helen, whose mother never ceases to be angry, berating her for every caring act she does; for Mary, who has the heartbreaking task of caring for a disabled adult child. (Of course, I've changed all their names because they don't need any more hassle.) I write for all those who have already chosen to be caregivers and are now wondering how they can stay the course and find some peace.

I have not included in the text of this book any comments from professionals or specialists or others who *seem* to have the credentials to give advice. (I have provided a bibliography at the end of the book if you should choose to read other things.) Simply reading another self-help book or consulting a professional will not provide the help we caregivers need for survival. I've tried that. Reading *this* book will not help you if you have not reached the point where you are ready to look inside yourself. But perhaps something I say will help you reach that point.

To find peace in the midst of turmoil, it is necessary to recognize that it is our own emotions that roil the waters. In the following chapters, I describe some of the changes in my own attitudes, which have brought me back from emotional exhaustion, but these are not changes that I say the caregiver *should* make. Caregivers do not need more *shoulds*. If my words make sense to you, if they bring you hope and point a way toward equilibrium, if they offer comfort, then accept them with my love and respect.

Chapter One

Accept Your Choice

You have chosen to be a caregiver. *Accept that choice.* When you truly believe that taking on this hard job is *your own choice*, you lift a burden of resentment that would otherwise eat away at you, eroding precious energy. Some of the caregivers I've talked to have protested, "But I *didn't* make this choice. There was nothing else I could do."

But that's not true. There is always something else we could do. The people who are not helping you—all those siblings and children and friends—have made a choice not to be caregivers. I have been going to the same nursing home for over fourteen years. I have seen patients there who never have visitors. I have even heard of families who were angry when they were contacted about a problem. "That's why she's in there," one family told the staff. "You're supposed to be handling that."

There's a difference between choosing to do something and wanting to do it. No one *wants* to take over the responsibility for another person's life. We certainly don't want to do the daily dirty chores that come with the disintegration of a body. We may not want to share the weird journeys of another's demented mind. Yet, because of something wonderful in you, you have looked past the distasteful things that you might not wish to do and have chosen to give care.

In the past few decades, some of the most beautiful words in the language have been tarnished by being associated with new, popular theories about mental health. Words such as nurture, cherish, share, give, and love have been mistakenly allied with such words as co-dependency, denial, weakness, and insecurity. Caregivers are often misunderstood simply because they have the courage and generosity to attempt to put another's interests ahead of their own. And society, dedicated to the idea that money and making it are the highest goods, gives lip service to caregivers but very little else. When a member of the Fortune 500 is honored for giving, it is always presented in figures—how much money did he give? There is no Fortune 500 list of those people who gave service down to the last bit of their energy and time. It is only in recent years that government has attempted to articulate the problems of caregivers, but most of the support is left up to volunteer organizations. To a great extent, society has walked away from those who need care.

Certainly, it is tempting to walk away. I tried very hard not to make the choice to care for my mother. There is a stage in the progress of diseases of dementia, such as Alzheimer's, where the patient is filled with fear, anger, and delusion; and like a wild wounded animal, the patient tends to strike out at whomever is nearest and dearest. My mother and I had been close friends and colleagues as writers. She was my first—and best—editor. I used to tease her and say that she wielded a "mean blue pencil," but her support meant a great deal to me. A published author herself, she was generous with her suggestions and time, not just in helping me but in helping others who came to her for advice and aid. She sponsored me for membership in my first professional organization, the Colorado Authors' League. She suggested markets, encouraged me to send stories out again when they had been rejected, offered help with re-writes, and was excited when I began to make sales—when the rejection slips slowly began to be replaced with letters of acceptance and then with checks.

When my first husband died, my mother was there to help with caring for my infant daughter. Many lonely weekends, I took the baby and went home to my parents' house to play Scrabble with my mother, to talk about writing, to feel encouraged. We spoke often on the phone, and when my parents were in another state, my mother and I wrote frequent letters. We were friends.

Then gradually, a change began. My mother did a few odd things— just minor things, different enough to cause comment between my father and the siblings, but not different enough to suggest any sort of major response. Mother was always very capable; and if she recognized a change in herself, she dealt with it in her way and went on teaching, taking care of the family's business, taking care of the home, and seeing to my father's failing health.

As my father's health continued to decline, Mother's actions became a little odder, a little more frantic, and slightly more irrational. She and my father returned to our home state, to a pleasant house in the small town they'd known as newlyweds fifty-five years before, hoping to find a place of peace.

But suddenly, as she struggled with caregiving herself, my mother moved into a wild nightmare of delusions and anger and irrational statements and actions. And suddenly, I became her villain. She began to complain to everyone that I was trying to take over her trust fund (a fund with which I'd never been associated, and which, at any rate, *she* had dissolved months before, using the funds to buy their house). She became violently jealous of my writing and angry when I had success (she who had, before this, gotten such a happy lilt in her voice when she was caring for my mail and found an acceptance there). She was suspicious of my activities in the Colorado Authors' League and began to believe that I was trying to undermine her career. Publication of my first novel brought her no joy.

My siblings, as confused as I was, would call me, after one of Mother's telephone tirades about me, and say, "What have you said to upset Mother?" Distressed and upset myself, I would say, "Nothing. Nothing. I haven't ever even mentioned her trust fund. I haven't done anything at CAL. I don't *know* why she says these things."

We blamed sleep deprivation. Mother was determined to give my father full-time care all by herself, and she was up day and night. But the delusions grew worse. She spoke of drug dealers in the crawlspace under her house and began to enlarge upon my involvement in these strange goings-on. A doctor where my father was hospitalized mentioned that she was showing signs of dementia, but we couldn't believe him. After all, Mother was caring for my father when he was at home. Her house was in order. The meals that she served were attractive and well balanced. Her checkbook was balanced as well. Only her wild, angry tirades on the phone about me to everybody who would listen were not in balance. I felt that she was using me as a safety valve of some sort, a way of releasing all the stress of her situation. But she refused any help with my father to ease the stress. All my siblings tried to help. I tried to help. She rejected us all, and my presence seemed to upset her the most.

Finally, all I could decide to do was withdraw. I kept in touch through my siblings, but I took little part in decisions made for her care or for my father's. After his death, my mother stoutly declared that she did not need grief counseling. My sister took her on a long trip to Africa to visit my brother. On her return, she had her home and her friends and her flowers. And we all hoped that she would now be able to devote time to her own writing, to building a life of her own.

But the dementia had a firm hold, and my mother's actions began to match her wild words. She drove off in her car to another state without telling anyone where she was going. Her driving in her hometown was erratic, and when the police stopped her, she lost her temper and her rationality. The police were sensitive, never taking her to jail, usually calling social services. She began to call 911 several times a day. Her fear of the noises in her crawlspace brought my sisters and brothers again and again to investigate. Aside from a few spider webs, nothing disturbed the empty, gravel-floored area under the house.

One night in January, when it was eight degrees below zero, my mother went to the neighbor's house to borrow some wire clippers. She wanted to cut the electric wires to her house to prevent drug dealers from traveling through the wires into her home. Alarmed, the neighbor called the police, and this time my mother was taken to a mental hospital for observation. The doctor diagnosed Alzheimer's disease.

It seems strange to me now that none of us had considered Alzheimer's disease. But at the time, we knew nothing about it. Fearful of adding to my mother's upset, I still stayed away. My sisters were reluctant to accept the doctor's diagnosis; they did not believe the nurse who told them that mother needed twenty-four-hour care. There was nothing out of order in her home or her business affairs to indicate that she was not in control of her life, despite the strange events that had taken her to the hospital.

Mother did not wish to live anywhere but in her own home. So my sisters took the difficult and emotional step of insisting that Mother give up her car keys when she went home from the hospital. They arranged for a woman to come in at mealtimes to help Mother and to give her the medicine the doctor had prescribed. They hoped that with some sedation, she would rest enough to be her old rational self—the capable mother to whom we had all turned so many times for solutions to our problems, for advice, for a loan, for reassurance, or just for a home-baked cinnamon roll and a cup of coffee.

Four days after the new arrangements had been made, my mother called me. In a voice devoid of anger, subdued, but more like the voice of my old friend, she told me that she didn't like the woman who was helping her. "Maybe," she said, her voice breaking a little, "maybe I'll come and visit you for awhile."

Startled, I was gentle but non-committal, and relieved when she hung up. I did not know that I wanted to take my mother into our home. I went for a walk in the woods on the mountain, and on my way back, I realized that I had made a decision. I chose to invite my mother for that visit. I chose to ask my husband to share the burden. I chose the best solution I could imagine in a bad situation. My decision was a relief, but there have been many, many times when I have had to remind myself that I made the choice.

And *you* have made the choice. Because you are able to put another's needs before your own, because you feel a sense of honor about taking responsibility for people in your sphere who cannot take responsibility for themselves, because you would not see your dear one left to the care of strangers, you have made the choice.

You need to accept that choice so that you can benefit from some of the positive emotions that go with the choice. One clear part of your mind, like a great cupboard of nourishment, can store the knowledge of your generosity, your integrity, your love, your strength, your courage, and your fortitude. You can give yourself the honor that society is so stingy in giving. Knowing that you have already stored such treasures by making the choice you did will help you through the terrible times when what you *chose* wars with what you *want*.

Accepting that choice allows you to release some of the stone-like emotions that weigh you down. You can stop dragging around your bag of resentment and self-pity. Nobody made you do this hard thing. There's no one to blame.

And because others stepped aside and by default allowed you to make that choice, they have given you a certain kind of freedom. Take that freedom. Each time you're tempted to worry about what others will think about what you do in your caregiving, each time someone tries to offer unwanted comments about what *they* would do, remind yourself that they did not make the choice. You made the choice. With a disease of dementia, no one really knows what is the totally right thing to do. But you made the choice to try to care for your demented person. (If you are dealing only with physical illness, there is a little more medical help, but you will still be the one making most of the decisions on a daily basis.) Knowing that you made the choice, and that you could have decided *not* to make that choice, will also help you release your anger at others who decided not to be the caregiver.

It amuses me now, in a situation that has few light moments, to use my clarity about choice to deal with those who think I should be doing things *their* way. Lighthearted, because I know what I chose and I know what they would *not* choose, I find it easy to say, "Well, if you see it that way, perhaps you would like to take over the caregiving for a week (a month, a year, for always)." Sometimes people surprise me and give a little help instead of a lot of advice, but mostly they back off and stop trying to mess with the routine I've established that enables me to meet the daily problems to the best of my ability.

Knowledge that you made the choice can give you direction and freedom in your actions, but there is a deeper knowledge that can inspire you and give you rest as you do the difficult tasks your choice has brought. Your choice tells a lot about the kind of person you are. And you can be proud of that person. Recognizing that you have strength, endurance, generosity, warmth, and a desire to help in this world is not a boastful thought. It is the truth about you that helped you make your choice to be a caregiver. Accept that choice.

Chapter Two

Release Your Relatives

For your own good, release your relatives from judgment and demands. I don't know your relatives. Perhaps they *are* acting in a way that, according to the majority opinion, deserves anger, censure, and reproof. When I suggest that you release your relatives, it is only because I know that the negative emotions they create in you are part of the unrelenting force that, like the constant surge of water against a sandbank, is eroding your well-being, threatening to wash away your ability to continue.

To ease your grim, exhausting need that your relatives should be doing something to help you, try to achieve the understanding that perhaps they truly *cannot* provide hands-on help.

All of us humans react oddly when faced with the intense emotions surrounding illness and loss. Those who have been widowed, for instance, are often advised to make no major changes for a year, because our emotions are in such turmoil that we don't know ourselves; we don't know what we will want to do with our lives; we haven't dealt with the details of the past.

The serious illness of a parent, child, or spouse causes many types of reaction. Each individual has a unique relationship with the patient. Even siblings raised in the same home, at the same time, have had different life experiences and different interaction with the parents and each other. Each responds in a different way to a crisis.

Some people go into denial. One of my sisters told me in recent years that when she heard the diagnosis of Alzheimer's disease at the hospital where my mother was treated, she simply refused to believe it. It did not seem possible to her that a woman who had so recently been caring for an ailing spouse and still running an apparently normal life could be the victim of dementia. At that time, since my sister didn't believe the diagnosis, she was unable to seek out and use information about the disease or to be informed and helpful in offering advice or care. One of my brothers, also in denial, asked other siblings, "Is it as bad as Elaine says it is?"

Some people are paralyzed by guilt. My brother-in-law had at one time told my mother that he would never see her placed in a nursing home. Now, later in life, fighting his own health problems, he was unable to make good on his promise to care for her. There is no promise so devastating when broken—whether it was asked for or given freely—as the vow never to let a dear one be institutionalized. Since some things are beyond our control, there are times when we absolutely cannot keep that promise.

Some people are hampered by fear. The sight of all the failing people in a nursing home may create such a sense of impending doom in a person, such knowledge of his own mortality, that he cannot face the idea of going to that place day after day to be part of caregiving.

Some people are still dealing with the past. They have not resolved their problems with the patient. Filled with anger and frustration, they cannot approach the patient without bringing along their emotional leftovers, and the pain of the unresolved makes them ineffective in helping you as the caregiver.

Since you have made the choice to be the caregiver, your mind is clearer than those of others in your sphere. You can think about your siblings, your children, and your other relatives in a less emotional manner.

At this point, you may be mad at *me* for even suggesting that your relatives shouldn't help you. I'm not saying that they shouldn't help you, but if they aren't going to help you, there's no point in enduring an angry whirlpool of emotions inside your own head, no point in trying to control other people, no point in arguments and bitter family infighting. You will be worn out and used up by your own emotions and those who *cannot* help still *will not* help.

Take a broader view of what you want. You want help now, of course. But in the future, when your patient has died, you will still want and need family. Creating an ongoing family feud with complaints, resentful harangues, and angry words will make it difficult later on to mend your relationships and find the comfort of a loving family circle.

It's better to find one good friend who will let you vent your feelings without broadcasting them to your family afterwards. And even with that friend, the sooner that you can stop depicting your relatives as villains, the better you will feel. You will release yourself from the exhaustion that comes from repeating and repeating negative emotions.

When I finally realized that my siblings could *not* help with the actual chores of caregiving, that knowledge freed me from several mental bonds and enabled me then to ask calmly, "Well, if you can't help with the hands-on care, what *can* you do?"

Having endured the pain of my mother's tirades about her trust fund, I could not face the thought of dealing with any of her money. While I could bathe her and change a diaper and try to soothe her irrational outbursts, when I had to open her checkbook, it made my stomach hurt. As we approached the court hearing for guardianship, I knew that I could not be conservator of her estate.

I asked one of my sisters, who had a full-time job as an executive assistant and was a thoughtful, capable businesswoman, if she would be willing to take on half the guardianship—the care of mother's money. She agreed, but the judge was doubtful. He was concerned that we would not be able to resolve conflicts when care cost a lot of money or when, as is now happening, the funds began to dwindle. We assured him that we could co-operate, and our unemotional united stance convinced him.

My other sister, who lives two thousand miles away, agreed to provide pretty clothes for our mother. The valley where I live has one small department store and one chain store, offering little choice for suitable, attractive clothes. I hate to shop, and I don't have time to drive the hundred miles to the nearest mall. But my mother is very much aware of what she wears. Pretty clothes raise her spirits. With information from me about what clothes could stand up under institutional laundering, my sister went shopping, and she has consistently provided lovely, coordinated, washable outfits. Her job is a very important one. Even though she is not close by, as far as I'm concerned, she is doing vital caregiving. And gratitude is a much easier emotion to harbor than resentment.

My older brother, who is now deceased, was hampered by a crippled leg, but he agreed to be with my mother when the court issued the summons that by law must be given to the patient when someone is suing for guardianship. He lived several hundred miles away, but he made the trip to our home, was tender and sympathetic as Mother read and understood and cried over the petition, which when acted upon would take away her personal freedom and choice. He stayed until after the court hearing and until we had moved her to a nursing home. He was also available for advice about medical decisions. There was much he could not do, but what he did was something that I needed.

My younger brother works in Africa. He cannot provide ongoing care. But when he is in the area, he visits Mother with an affectionate, relaxed, practical manner that cheers her and gives her a sense that her family circle is larger than that provided by my visits.

We didn't come to these accommodations easily. We came to them through grief and pain. I struggled with my emotions and wept and raged and wore my husband out and wore myself out, feeling over-burdened and resentful. And *nothing* was different in the end than it would have been had I accepted the realities of the situation from the very first day.

Giving my relatives freedom from my demands gave me freedom from *their* demands. Since I am in charge of my mother's care, I don't ask permission of anyone, nor do I spend time with the guilty feeling that I *should* have done this or I *ought* to do that because someone said so. Only once have I had to impose restrictions using my legal guardianship. Realizing that I could do that gave me a sense of calm that allows me to consult with my family without rancor.

We spend a lot of time in our world trying to find someone to blame for the problems in our lives. It is exhausting. Caregivers are always tired anyhow. Releasing our relatives is one more restful step toward peace.

Chapter Three

Know the Patient

It seems like odd advice to tell you to know someone you've known all your life, or all her life, or all your married years. But in our society, the moment someone becomes seriously ill, we go into a kind of sentimental haze about them. Suddenly, the patient becomes "courageous, valiant, a wonderful human being." Or else, the patient becomes "the elderly ill or the disabled," losing all personality and uniqueness. Television human-interest stories almost always take this condescending tone. We use fuzzy thinking and get emotional just at the moment when we need to be absolutely honest. We do this especially with mothers. In recent years, there have been books about problems with our mothers, but in the mythology we are all forced to live with, there is still a pedestal set tall for mothers. If we didn't have a perfect mother, we dream of one. We don't see mothers as real human beings with strengths and weaknesses.

And with all patients—parents, spouses, children—we tend to see only what they have *lost*, not what they have retained that will help with their care. We come to caregiving with a serious intent to help another person, but sometimes by taking too much control away from that person, we only hinder his well-being.

Who is this person with whom you are now forced to be even more intimate? First, just because we see the ill person as different from the well person, we need to ask, who *was* this person?

My mother was and is a fascinating, talented, intelligent, persistent, sometimes erratic, sometimes maddening, often endearing, often humorous, sometimes desperate, and always complicated human being.

She was born on a small ranch in northeastern Colorado in 1909, three years after her parents had each taken a homestead and married with the intent of joining their lands and their lives. But hard times sent her father out to work for others while her mother stayed on the ranch—driving a horse-drawn wagon as a school bus, selling eggs and milk for cash income, and finally acting as the postmistress for the small town of Iliff, while continuing to run the ranch. My grandmother was a thrifty woman of German heritage. She had been a teacher before her marriage, and she herself was a complicated mixture of practicality and dreams. My mother used to ride, as a toddler and small child, on the saddle in front of her mother while they went to the pastures to tend cows. While they rode, my grandmother quoted poetry to the child—long, many-versed adults poems, which my mother memorized and was able to quote for years later, up to the time when the Alzheimer's disease stole her ability to find words. But she also learned her mother's bitterness over an often-absent husband and father, who could not seem to provide for the family or practice the German thrift his wife felt was called for.

My mother grew up on a horse, riding the river bottoms of the South Platte to help keep track of the family's cattle. She did not like the household tasks set to her by her careful mother. She went roaming when she could to keep from picking up her needle and thread or spending time in the kitchen. But under her mother's stern guidance, she learned to do all the chores expected of a woman in those days. She cooked and baked, made clothes and darned socks, killed and cleaned chickens, milked cows, churned butter, cleaned house, washed clothes on the board and dried them on the line then ironed them with flatirons heated on the wood stove. She tended garden, canned the produce from the garden, went to school, and went to church.

But she also sneaked out of the house at night to sit under the bunkhouse windows and listen to the cowboys talk. She went watermelon-stealing and played tricks on the owner of the watermelon patch. She survived a late-night wreck when the Model-T she was riding in turned over in a ditch. She began to write verse, usually irreverent and funny, but sometimes wistful and searching. She played high-school basketball. She graduated at the age of fifteen and went to the University of Colorado, where she joined the CU hiking club and with that group went hiking and climbing. They were a carefree band who often did reckless things, such as skiing by moonlight on an unmarked mountain trail.

Mother left the university after two years and took a teaching job at a tiny school on the Colorado prairies, riding a horse ten miles to start the morning fire in the schoolhouse and riding the horse back again to the teacher's residence after a day of dealing with a mixture of students, several of whom were older and larger than she was. For social life, she and the other teachers attended the area dances held in schoolhouses, sometimes in barns. She met my father at a dance on New Year's Eve in 1929 and eloped with him on April 11, 1930, keeping her marriage a secret from the school board until the end of the school year, lest she lose her job.

Determined that her children would not be separated from their father as she had been, she followed her husband as he struggled to support a family through the Depression years, living in hired hands' cabins on various ranches. One year she left their oldest son with her mother so he could go to school and took the other three small children to a house trailer with no running water at a highway construction site. Her husband worked a night shift. Desperately lonely, she wrote her mother lengthy letters, full of longing to see her son and humorous verse through which she attempted to ease her distress over her primitive living conditions. She could not leave her children to ride in the moonlight, to dance, to explore.

She created a many-layered life in her mind, and some of the layers were hidden even from herself. Occasional storms of emotion would erupt, spewing out a volcanic flow of distress and anger. She began to develop a habit of finding a villain outside herself whom she could blame for her circumstances in some way. Later in her life, people would suggest that she was mildly paranoid. She also turned to strangers and outsiders to feed the need she had for the exotic, the different—anything that eased the feeling she had of being trapped in the mundane. People were drawn to her. Many a Sunday dinner was expanded by her to include drop-ins—relatives, friends, acquaintances. She was torn between the domestic and the distant. Her poems bore titles such as "Gypsy Song." She began to send a few of them out to markets.

During a five-year period of living in Denver before and after World War II, Mother joined a writers' group, sent out more stories and poems, and was published enough to be accepted into the Colorado Authors' League. And then, following her husband once more, she moved her children to a lonely ranch to live in another ranch hand's house with no electricity, no bathroom, and only a pump at the sink to provide water. The ranch was too remote to be on the school bus route, so morning and evening, even when the prairies were hidden in blizzards, she drove her children to another ranch to meet the bus. Desperate for more life of the mind, and lonely once more as her husband worked long hours and was often too tired at the end of the day to tune into her needs, she found a small group of writers in a large town even farther away and drove the miles at night after her day's chores to attend the writers' meetings.

Finally, her need for *more* forced a crisis in the family. "I want my children to go to college, to have a chance at a broader life." The family left the prairies and moved to the mountains. To supplement her husband's salary, she found work as a teacher, although she had no degree. Then, after thirty-seven years away from college, she went back to school and graduated with a four-point average from the University of Denver.

For many years, she taught school, kept house, took in relatives, listened to friends, chose villains, loved her husband, fought *with* and *for* her children, stole away for a ten-minute adventure when she went for groceries and supplies, and talked to strangers for a glimpse of a larger life.

Teaching became as important as writing. She taught in Colorado, Wyoming, and Arizona. At the age of sixty-seven, she was still teaching small children. After that, she taught the profoundly mentally retarded in an Arizona school. She earned many citations for excellence in teaching. Her writing also won awards. She was listed in *Who's Who in Colorado*.

She saw her children through college. She remained devoted to her husband. They held hands at the table, continued to go dancing, centered their attention on each other. As his health deteriorated, she went with him to another far out ranch, this one in Wyoming, seeking a less stressful life for him. When that was not the place, she went with him to the desert and then to the seashore.

When her husband died, back in the town where they had started, after sixty-one years of marriage, when she could have been free to seek out a larger life of her own, she was already used up and well into dementia. Nothing was left for herself. She was filled with fear, which surfaced as uncontrollable anger.

This was the woman whom we chose to take into our home and care for. My husband had not known the woman I've just described. He came into the picture when she was already showing the first mild signs of dementia. In our home, Mother felt all the desperation of being in the last place where she could go before being confined to an institution. With all the persistence that she had shown in surviving through the Depression, in seeing that her children were educated, in caring for her husband until his death, she resisted the inevitable deterioration of her life. But now her perseverance, her persistence, came through only as stubborn fury. My husband saw the fear and anger, the hysteria, and did not see how we could survive.

I have not presented this long description of my mother to show that she is different. I have presented it to show that while she is unique in her own way, she is *not* different from your patient. All humans respond with anger or depression when they are afraid. All humans have double-sided traits. Perseverance can be stubbornness. Rich emotion can be so intense that it frightens others. Good organization may become a rigid habit. And so on.

Your patient is unique too, and equally complex. You need to know all the strengths and weaknesses so that you can calmly use the strengths and reach a loving hand to soothe the fear brought on by the weaknesses. When some erratic action occurs, you can ask, "Is this the disease, or is this just a trait of Mother's, heightened by the disease?"

In order to meet my mother's deepest needs, in order to tap into her remaining strengths, in order to ease the fears that erupted into anger, I had to really *know* my mother. I needed to review every loving, caring, generous thing she'd ever done and call on those positive aspects of her character, but I couldn't look away from the times in which she had been emotional, volatile, and erratic. I could not blame the disease for her unpleasant traits. I could not assume that all Alzheimer's patients are demented in the same way. I could not let my mother become a generic term—an "Alzheimer's victim."

Knowing my mother's interests, I could set up her environment to reflect them. Along with the usual family photos on her bulletin board, I put a heading that said, "Evelyn is a poet and a teacher." Beneath the heading, I posted several of her poems. One morning during the earlier stages of the disease, she said to me, "I like that bulletin board. It helps me when I wake up and don't know who I am." Working with the staff at the nursing home, I provided her favorite poems and other poems that, while she could still read, she read aloud to the other residents.

Sometimes, knowing my mother well helped me give the staff suggestions about activities. They said, "She won't work in coloring books. She doesn't like staying in the lines." Well, of course not. She's spent a lifetime trying to stay in the lines to suit everyone else. Now, released from the world's expectations, she is free to wander, even on paper. We decided to try finger painting and other forms of art less confining.

The staff said, "She can't do complicated things, but she won't play games that seem as if they are for children." Of course not. She is The Teacher, and she does not respond well to being treated like a child. One of her most exasperating habits is that of grasping a fellow resident and trying to make him go inside if he's outside or settle down somewhere if he's moving. She still feels, and used to state, that she must control and see to the welfare of the "children." It's easier to deal with her inappropriate attempts at control if you see them with her history in mind.

She loves words and ideas. As she began to lose the use of simple words, she would often substitute more complicated ones. She reads signs. She reads nametags. In the beginning of her stay at the nursing home, she could still read magazines and books. When she couldn't understand what I *said* to her, she could still read notes and respond with great intelligence and depth. We spent many happy hours during my visits communicating through my written notes and her spoken answers. One sad day, she looked at a note and said, "I can read the sentence, but I don't know what it means." But she still responded for a while to written words. The staff and I provided flashcards with pictures of animals and a one-word name. Mother would concentrate on those cards and say the name, an activity she seemed to enjoy so much that she would cease her wandering and stay put for half an hour.

My mother loves to go for a ride. I've taken her into the hills and onto the plains. Sand Lake is loud with the greetings from geese and ducks; a meadow along Highway 291 is filled with mares and colts in the spring; a small herd of deer lives in the local cemetery. There is a place where the Arkansas River runs close to a country road. Even now, when my mother is often unable to respond with speech, she will smile and nod if I say, "Shall we go for a ride?" Diminished by disease, she is not changed. The gypsy stills sings in her soul.

She loves children. Sometimes just going to a playground is an outing that gives her joy. Her face lights up at the sight of children anywhere. We encourage young grandchildren and nieces and nephews to visit.

She enjoys strangers, and her intense interest in them attracts smiles and focus from others. Sometimes she will attempt to talk to a stranger and resist moving on. This can be very trying, but it helps if one is aware that some of her needs were *always* met by strangers. If you and the stranger can both be patient for a few moments, she will finally release you both, and you will know that you have provided an "activity" suited to her needs.

For the first five years of her confinement at the nursing home, my mother was still trying to take care of my father. She asked about him, looked for him, and resisted any suggestion that he was dead. When a male resident was moved into the ward, my mother began to call him by my father's name, to reach for his hand, to attempt to take care of him in inappropriate ways. It is extremely difficult for a child, even an adult child, to enter into the private world of a parent's sexual and emotional needs. *Knowing* my mother helped me through this trying time.

My mother could voice her needs only through the structure she had set up and lived in for a lifetime—marriage to my father. That first male resident, who had problems of his own, was moved to another facility, but Mother reacted in a similar demonstrative manner to other male residents, one of whom was more predatory. Knowing that she would have been humiliated at any time in her life by an unsavory situation, I was able to be firm, but calm, in my insistence that she and that particular male be separated.

The situations that arise in caring for a demented patient, or any patient, may be exhausting in themselves; but if the caregiver approaches them in a confused manner because she doesn't know what the patient's own desires are, they become overwhelming. It takes mental work to study another human being so intensely, but the reward of such work is a basic clarity about the person that gives the caregiver a reliable standard for action.

Clarity in one's own mind is very freeing. The work of caregiving is still to be done, but the stress of the work is much relieved when you know the patient.

Chapter Four

Know Yourself

There are a million people to tell you what you *should* do. Only you know what you *can* do. But to protect yourself from all those suggestions, comments, demands, and complaints, you need to understand your own strengths and weaknesses.

First, we caregivers need to understand that we were probably programmed in childhood to pick up some of the burdens we think we've freely taken upon ourselves. In many families, there is one child designated to shoulder the family burden to "make things better." It is usually a female child, but there are also male children who have carried for their whole lives the impossible assignment of making things better for everyone in the family. Depending upon our temperament, when we are told to be a "good little girl," we kick over the traces and become a "bad little girl," we become an "indifferent little girl," or we take on the chore of being a "good little girl" and endure it by suppressing our need for our own freedom and by finding compensation in the approval given to good girls.

Because nobody in the family actually knows what is needed to "make things better," the child faces an impossible task. In attempting to solve every problem, ease every painful emotion, and understand adult subtleties, the child is taking a complicated course with no syllabus and no teacher for guidance. Though the child is usually feeling tense and stressed, there is no designated person to make *her* feel better, and so she puts up a front of caring and cheerfulness. The caregivers I know do a lot of laughing, but if you talk to them one-on-one and invite their real feelings, the laughter turns to tears.

The family that has so programmed a child is conflicted in its feelings about the efforts the child puts forth to make things better. Family members are willing to take what the willing child gives, but they know, deep down, that it is not fair to take so much. Their guilt makes them feel resentful of that child. And because the child is heavily relied on by the parents, the siblings may see that child as "closer" to the parents and may resent that too.

Not understanding the undercurrents, the child usually just tries harder, increasingly taking over responsibilities that belong to other people, incurring more resentment. When everyone in the family reaches adulthood, the siblings may still want to take, but may also resent the intensity of the caregiver's efforts to give. The parents may become even more clinging, refusing to validate the caregiver's attempts to have a life of her own. And, especially as they age or become ill, their fears may make them reach clutching hands toward the child who was supposed to make things better.

If a caregiver is lucky, and has a few wise helpers along the way, she can begin to see the family pattern. With deep, hard emotional work, she can place limits on what she is willing to do, to recognize the limits that are inherent in any situation, and to acknowledge the problems about which she can do absolutely nothing. She can separate the efforts she wishes to make of her own free will from the efforts she feels coerced into doing, and she can then make healthy responses.

There is true joy in caring for others, but it does not come from blindly accepting the family's designation. That joy comes from recognizing that you have a skill for listening and caring and nurturing and nursing; that joy comes from using those skills. It comes from seeing a larger picture than the family, from understanding that the world is a much nicer place when people *care,* and that to be a caregiver of one's own free will is a rewarding activity. To look for the joy of caregiving in other people's appreciation and affirmation is probably going to lead to disappointment. The patient is often too miserable, too conflicted by loss of autonomy, to appreciate the one who takes over his care. The family often feels too guilty and too involved in the tangle of lifelong relationships to offer affirmation to the caregiver.

Once you have a little understanding of how you got where you are, what made you make the choice, you will feel freer to decide each day just what you want to do in the complicated role you've chosen. When we do something we don't like to do, we are going to be more tense and become exhausted more quickly. Even in such a seemingly grim setting as a nursing home, there are choices one can make between what's pleasant and what's draining.

I don't like to operate through a group. I much prefer to go directly to a primary source to find information. I like face-to-face discussion. I am impatient with organized presentations. Institutions are invested in organized everything. Social service directors and public relations directors try very hard to get me involved in the groups created by the institution. One of the most freeing things I've learned is that I *don't have to do what I don't want to do.* If I don't want to stay at the nursing home to attend a group meeting after I've visited with my mother, if I don't want to drive the sixty-four miles again at night after I've already been at the institution, I just don't do it. I don't make excuses, I don't apologize, I don't suggest that I'll do it next time, I don't think about my refusal after I've given it. What a huge bundle of unnecessary emotion I can dump right there. I respect the people who operate through groups, but I recognize that they made that choice, and I made a different one.

You may find a great sense of relief in joining a group and sharing your concerns with others. *You* might want a more structured approach to learning about the disease and the care of your patient. The point is that if you know what *you* want, you can set aside all those things that you don't want, those demands that cause stress and drain your emotions.

There are some parts of personal caretaking that I find difficult. When she was in our home I could bathe my mother, change her diapers, do her laundry, and change her bed, but I just could not bring myself to clean her teeth. We both felt that it was an invasive action. Even on the days when she would look at the toothbrush and ask, "What's that for?";

even on the days that she took the toothbrush loaded with toothpaste and carefully brushed her lips or her face, I could not brush her teeth. It made me gag, it made us both tense, and it put me in a horrible mood. I stayed in much better humor by patiently coaxing her, by demonstrating what *she* should do, and I was usually more successful in reaching the goal of a clean mouth for her than if I tried to clean it myself. I made appointments for her with a dentist and had her teeth cleaned regularly, but I did not brush her teeth. After we moved Mother from our home, a wonderful dental hygienist agreed to come regularly to the nursing home to clean Mother's teeth, and I applaud and encourage the staff members who help with her tooth brushing. I don't pick on myself because I cannot do that service.

Another thing I know about myself: I don't like to be criticized. Some folks can roll criticism off their backs and never let it affect their emotions, but I can't. Since I'm usually trying as hard as I can to please every damned body, criticism feels like an extra load. It is even painful when it comes from the demented patient, who may not know what she's saying or may be dumping inner feelings that have nothing to do with me. What do I do about it? Well, first I try to be quiet and give myself time to think and become calm. Then I try to be honest about the situation. Is the criticism helpful? That's all that really matters. Will a change on my part improve the caregiving situation, help the patient, or help me? If the answer is yes, I consider the suggestions. Otherwise, I picture a large wastebasket and mentally dump all the criticism into it. Sometimes I picture a trash truck in which I dump the criticism. I want all that unnecessary negative emotion hauled away so I won't retrieve it and go over it again and again. People who criticize you often mask it as suggestions intended to help. But if criticism makes you feel bad, no matter the face it wears, dump it. You don't need it.

I hate to be in the presence of two people at the same time and to be torn between their needs and demands. One of the hardest parts of having both a husband and a mother in the same house was that each needed my attention, each had emotions about the other, each had opinions about the situation, and each felt that I belonged solely to him or her.

Caring for two people in the same place at the same time is difficult. My mother was at her clearest early in the morning, so I tried to focus on her then and achieve some real communication. After she was in bed, for the two hours that she would sleep before waking and getting up to roam around again, I would visit with my husband and focus on his needs. And in mid-afternoon, I left them together and went for a walk in the woods to focus on *my* needs.

We tried having someone come in to stay for a while with Mother so that we could get away, but there are few people who understand enough about Alzheimer's disease to deal with a patient safely, especially one as strong willed as my mother. One time, we took my mother to the home of a woman who was caring for other Alzheimer's patients, but my mother was terrified by the strange surroundings and ran away. It took hours to calm her down when she was at home again.

As we went through these experiences, I had an eye on my own physical and mental condition, and there came a day when I knew that I could not continue to go without sleep, and I could not deal day and night with the stress of Mother's disease and its effects on my husband. I had to make a change before our situation became tragic. Because I knew myself, I did not feel guilty about making the change.

One of the most difficult things to deal with when you are trying to know yourself and do what is right for you is the true concern for your welfare expressed by kind and loving friends who think that they know you and can speak for what you need. It has been difficult to explain to friends that I do not need a night out with them. Because I am emotionally empty, having to respond in a social situation, having to listen and sympathize, or even letting others listen to my troubles is not something that will fill my empty well.

Giggling with my granddaughter fills my needs. Flying for two hours over the mountains, where my entire mind must be focused on the controls of the airplane and the conditions of the air, is refreshing. Learning more demanding chords on my guitar helps me feel renewed. Hiking and snowshoeing, which both demand a lot physically but not emotionally, are ways I know to renew my energies. (Reading fiction used to be a pleasure, but lately the tragedies of the lives I see in the nursing home are so much more compelling than fiction that I cannot get involved in a plot.)

You will want to find your *own* ways of keeping up your emotional strength. You are the only one who knows what your schedule is and what makes you feel good. You don't need to do what I do. You don't need to take suggestions from me or anyone else. You have the right to know yourself and to enjoy what gives you relaxation and a sense of freedom and renewed energy to go on with your caretaking job.

If you don't feel peaceful and joyous, then the situation is not recreation, no matter what others may call it. If you know yourself, you'll learn where to find your own peace.

Chapter Five

Know the Disease

Dealing with any kind of disease is frustrating because no patient reacts in the same way to a disease. Medications do not have the same effect on one patient as on another. When the patient is not aware, or not informed, the burden of understanding the disease falls upon the caregiver. Quite often, the doctor depends upon the caregiver to be alert to changes and anomalies.

After my husband's heart attack, I asked for and received from the American Heart Association information about heart disease and the part diet, particularly cholesterol, plays in it. We bought and learned to use a blood-pressure monitoring machine. To deal with his gout, we consulted a specialist in arthritic diseases who did tests to make sure that he had real gout and then prescribed medication. We also consulted the dietician at a local hospital to learn which foods increase the uric acid level in the body, since a high uric acid level contributes to gout. She was gracious and helpful, and she charged no fee. When my husband was further diagnosed with diabetes, we obtained information from the Diabetes Association and with advice from a doctor bought and learned to use a glucose-monitoring machine. I read all the printouts that came with the medications and asked questions of the pharmacist.

When a drug prescribed to control his angina began to cause side effects in my husband's body, we did not at first suspect the drug because those side effects were not listed in the printout about common side effects. But because we knew and understood the readings on the various monitoring devices, we were able to see that the blood pressure and glucose levels were under control. We could eliminate some of the medicines because they had not caused trouble before. We could not know, however, if the drugs, working in combination, were causing the weakness, loss of muscle tone, fatigue, and pain he was experiencing. We asked the arthritis doctor if he thought the medications might be causing the problem. He did not think they were.

But because I was in the situation every day and could study my husband, I finally decided that his symptoms were not part of *any* disease. I went to our pharmacist and asked her for more complete information about the drugs he was using, and through her careful searching, she found a brochure that listed as side effects of a particular drug all the symptoms my husband was experiencing. Only a small percentage of people suffer those side effects, not even enough to put the warning on the regular printout.

We consulted with the heart doctor, who gave directions about stopping the medication and how to deal with angina in the absence of the medicine. Within three weeks, the symptoms began to disappear.

As the caregiver, knowing the diseases I was dealing with helped me spot something out of the ordinary. Knowing what to expect, knowing whom to call, knowing how to record pertinent information, knowing what a doctor would want to know—all this knowledge eased some of the stress of a grave situation.

The caregiver is the only coordinator between various doctors, nursing staff, pharmacist, and organizations. Often the patient is too ill, as in my husband's case, or too confused, as in my mother's case, to know and understand the disease and the medication.

Conversation with your doctor may be helpful, if he has time to speak with you alone. My doctor offered information about my situation when I was caring for Mother at home, but it was during a time when he was examining my mother and I was occupied trying to keep her calm. Because of my own distress, I had to ask that the doctor repeat the information. Then, I asked when I would know that I couldn't keep her at home any longer. He said, "Most people make the move to a nursing home when the patient loses control of bowels and bladder. Homes are not set up to deal with the cleaning and laundry work required to care adequately for the patient." One other negative, but still helpful, comment he made—"You will wear out before your mother does"—reminded me to be alert in monitoring my own physical condition. I will always be grateful to that doctor for recommending the book *The Thirty-Six Hour Day*, which provides a comprehensive view of diseases of dementia.

Now that Mother is in a nursing home, and after several changes in physicians (because it's hard to keep doctors in this more remote area), we finally have a young doctor who seems to understand Alzheimer's disease and who works with me to keep Mother comfortable even though we cannot stop the progression of the disease. We communicate through letters so that we don't play telephone tag and so that we can give coherent reports of the situation. The doctor often asks my opinion of Mother's condition, since I see her more often than he does. I also help as a liaison between the doctor and the nursing home staff. I always provide a copy of my letter to the doctor for Mother's file so that the duty nurse and others can see what I've said and we can coordinate the care.

Making written records is a little more work, but it is a great relief from trying to remember data when I'm dealing with Mother and the doctor at the same time in his office, and it causes far less emotional stress to organize the information at my own pace, when I am rested, and then submit it to the doctor for him to consider at his convenience.

It is important to write down the doctor's instructions, especially about the dosage of medicine. We kept an index card with current instructions for the use of Arthur's prescriptions near the medicine as a vital aid to being sure that I administered it properly. Most caregivers are not registered nurses, but many of the duties they perform are those of registered nurses. When something is written down, you needn't try to remember it. When you are tired, as caregivers usually are, it is easier to make mistakes if one is counting on one's memory. And should any unforeseen event occur, written records are always more accurate than memory and better meet the needs of government officials.

In getting to know a disease, it is important for your own sake to go beyond the official information. The official information gives you the scientific overview, but only the people who have dealt with a disease can give you the *unscientific unpleasant* realities and help you find successful ways of dealing with those realities. It is in this area that a support group made up of people who have dealt hands-on with the disease is of most help. Every person who has cared for an Alzheimer's patient at any stage of the disease can give you some piece of information about the disease, its progression, and the way a patient may act at each level. Every piece of useful information about the actual working out of the disease will prepare you to deal with the next crisis in a better informed, calmer, less confused, and more peaceful way. So even if you are like I am and don't find it restful to attend group meetings, when you are first learning about Alzheimer's disease, you can get a lot of real information very quickly by attending a family support group and listening to the stories told by people who have been dealing with a patient longer than you have.

The staff in the Alzheimer's unit is also a valuable source of information. Listen to what the staff tells you about your own patient, work with them in adjusting to changes, and take their advice. The staff has the advantage of seeing the disease in many stages at once among their various patients and can offer wonderfully comforting guidance.

You will find great joy in the state of mind that comes with knowing as much as you can about the disease. When you are confident in your knowledge, you aren't stressed as much by the fear that you will do the wrong thing. Family/staff conferences are of much more value if you feel that you understand staff comments and can respond to them in an informed manner.

Knowing the disease helps you to ease your family's distress as well. If you understand the level your patient has reached, you can prepare visitors and guide them toward a successful interaction with the patient. Knowing the patient, you can also help visitors overcome difficulties that are *not* caused by Alzheimer's. My mother is quite deaf, but she reads lips well. The simple act of making sure that Mother is looking at your face when you speak to her often results in surprising communication.

It takes a lot of effort to do so much research, especially at a time when you are trying to care for another person as well as yourself. But after the initial effort, the work is less difficult, while the rewards—peace of mind, confidence, and competence—are immense.

Chapter Six

Get Rid of Guilt

We met at the door of the nursing home and exchanged a polite "How are you?" A woman of my age, she was caring for an ailing husband at home and trying to meet the needs of her mother in the facility. In answer to my greeting she said, "I feel so guilty. I need to be at home, but my mother complains that I don't spend enough time with her. How do you deal with that guilty feeling?"

This same woman had asked me questions before, and I felt some responsibility as a "mentor." I took a moment to consider my reply. Moving to one side so that a nurse pushing a wheel chair could exit, I said to the troubled woman, "There are three parts to this equation, and you can't get the answer without considering all three—your husband, your mother, and *you*. You are as much a person as the other two. If something happens to you—if you become so worn and distressed that you can't care for them—they will both suffer; but you will suffer as well, and you are every bit as important as the people for whom you are caring. Your mother is safe and warm and well fed and provided with a caring staff. Since she still has her mental faculties, she can use the recreational opportunities provided. You visit regularly. There is no reason for you to feel guilty simply because someone complains."

My comments sounded somewhat cold to me, but the smile on the woman's face told me that I had said something helpful. Words, however, cannot always help eradicate the feeling of guilt.

Guilt is a perfectly acceptable and protective emotion when we've acted in an unloving or hurtful way or broken one of the rules that help to keep society functioning. If we've lied, cheated, stolen, or been other-wise destructive, our conscience is a blessed corrective which guides us to actions that will repair the damage we've done and protect the social structure that enables us all to cooperate and to progress toward mutual happiness. We are all, as a part of humanity, responsible for our share of the plan, and we can use guilt over our actions to guide us.

But the kind of guilt that we so often feel—the guilt for what we *haven't* done—is like a rat gnawing at our insides. None of us feels that we are perfect; most of us feel that we *ought* to be perfect. Nobody knows what perfection is. Possibly, when the huge mosaic of life is put together, with each of us fitting into our own little space, the result might be close to perfection. But that vague, nagging guilty feeling does not light the way to perfection. It just wears us out.

Probably each of us caregivers could use some therapy to understand and deal with our feelings of guilt, but I know very few caregivers who have the time, money, access to professional help, or emotional stamina to go into therapy while they're attempting to meet the needs of their patients. The best we can do is to shine the light of common sense and honesty on that shadowy place where guilt resides and see if we can at least reduce it to a gnawing mouse.

One of the first things a caregiver needs to realize is that *she did not cause the condition of the patient.* Because of early training, because of unselfish caring, because of the vows that she made, the caregiver has agreed to take on the care of another person, but nothing about that agreement implies that the caregiver created the disease. That is one pos-sible source of guilt that is dissipated by common sense.

A second honest thought that helps to stop the gnawing feeling is that *no one is truly responsible for another's life.* Parents of small children are responsible for the care and guidance of a child as it develops, but even that child, from birth, is a separate person with its own fingerprints, voiceprint, DNA, personality, and heritage. We are all part of a larger unity—humanity—but each of us plays out his own part. As I try to speak for my mother's welfare where she can't speak for herself, I am still aware that her life is her own. I cannot live it for her, I cannot suffer her disease for her, I cannot accompany her in her dying. It is not my responsibility to attempt any of those impossible things. And common sense tells me that there is no point in feeling guilty about something that is not my responsibility.

Common sense also tells me that *I can only do what I can do.* I was not dealing with my husband's condition or my mother's illness as a perfected human being with all the answers. I am a person with my own fears, my own aches and pains and sorrows, my own history. I can act, using the skills and wisdom I have, in whatever condition I am at a particular time. If I'm feeling down and incompetent one day, I need to recognize that there is a flow and an ebb in human abilities and emotions. I will be up and very competent another day. If one attempted solution doesn't work, I may have another inspiration and the next attempt may be successful. But guilt over any supposed failure is only going to make the down time last longer.

If I'm thoroughly honest and not off on some ego trip, I will accept the fact that *I am only a part of the care plan.* There are doctors, nurses, aides, administrative staff, relatives, friends, government officials, receptionists, accountants, pharmacists, dentists, hygienists, housekeepers, medical supply staff, dieticians, maintenance men, and dozens and dozens of others involved in the care of my mother. Arthur had his own health force of doctors, pharmacists, therapists, and hospice nurses. Both Mother and Arthur had some sort of relationship with each of those people.

My mother has always greeted the staff, including the man who comes to fix the plumbing and the one who fills the Coke machine. Even when her verbal abilities diminished, she tried to connect with people in the facility. All these people are part of the care plan, and because each of them provides something my mother needs, I do not take on the burden of feeling that it is all up to me, with the accompanying guilt should I find myself unable to meet some demand. I am not giving care in a vacuum.

It is not unkind to recognize that the patient has determined throughout her life how to live that life, including the way of dealing with illness and hard times. People choose along the way to indulge in habits that may cause illness, to develop emotional responses that make it difficult for others to help them, and to create situations that lead to discomfort. On the other hand, some people choose habits that help them when trouble comes. My parents both had a sense of independence that could be exasperating, but it was obvious to all their children that they had chosen to be rugged individualists for as long as they could be. When the time comes to help people, one cannot feel guilty about the way they chose to live their lives. A whiner or a complainer will be even more of a whiner when the trials of old age come along. I am pleased with my mother for her determination to stay as alive as possible. She is not a complainer. She used to say, "If we just fly right in," we can get this done … or fix that … or make things better. Despite the ravages of Alzheimer's, she is still independent and brave, and she still fights for the things that make her feel that way. Sometimes, when we return from a ride, she refuses to get out of the car. I can only assume that her reason is a need not to give up the joy of being a gypsy, of being out and about. It is frustrating to deal with her actions, but I am proud of her emotions. Even while I'm feeling aggravated, I want to cheer and say, "Thatta girl! Hang in there! Fight for what you need!"

I save a little of that cheer for me. Sometimes I have to take a day for what *I* need. It happens that what I need is rather expensive. An hour of flying, especially if I take my friend and flight instructor along, is a real indulgence given our budget. But an hour of flying and a morning of talk with the other pilots at the airport is as good as a two-week vacation, which I *can't* take, and so I am shameless and guilt free as I spend the money. I'm equally shameless at hinting to all my relatives that I'd prefer "flying money" to any other Christmas or birthday gift. There are cheaper indulgences. One of the caregivers I know was looking very discouraged, and when I asked if she was all right, she burst out, "I hate my hair." She was worried about money, about the cost of caring for her husband, and even though her son had told her to go to a hairdresser if she wanted to, she felt too guilty to do it. I pointed out that half the assets of a marriage belong to the wife and that she was probably not taking anywhere near her share—that she was definitely entitled to go to a hairdresser once a week. She smiled and gave me a hug, and I noticed a few days later that she had a new and attractive haircut. When I told her how pretty she looked, she blushed and smiled and voiced no guilt.

Sometimes we hesitate to give up our guilty feelings and our martyred actions because we don't want to seem cold and uncaring. We don't want others to think less of us or to consider us "selfish." Martyrdom, according to my Webster's dictionary, is "the suffering of death for adhering to a belief, faith, or profession." Common sense and honesty tell us that a dead person is no help to anyone else, even if she's only emotionally dead.

If you can do something in any situation, *do it* and feel good about it. If you can't do it, that's okay, because if you can't do it, it's not your job anyway. If it really needs doing, someone else will do it. The useless gnawing rat of guilt can eat up your confidence and your self-esteem and your joy. Give up your guilt.

Chapter Seven

Away with Anger

Anger is a selfish, destructive, useless emotion that can destroy your peace of mind faster than any other emotion. Although we in our society have addressed millions of words to the subject of anger, we are not comfortable with it. We've been told to control it, own it, vent it, share it, shout it, analyze it, act it, write it down, write it up, and write it out, and we justify it sometimes by calling it "righteous." We very seldom read or hear the suggestion that we might be healthier and more nearly whole if we simply didn't have anger.

Most people's reaction to that suggestion is that it is impossible not to have anger. It is difficult, perhaps, but it is not impossible if you're willing to change your mind. If you're not willing to change your mind, you won't find the peace you're looking for, because trying to be peaceful while harboring anger is like trying to mop the floor while a volcano is erupting in your kitchen.

We need, first, to verbalize our anger in a different way. We need to stop using the emotion with the verb *to be*. We often say I *am* angry. That makes the anger part of us, part of our being. It is much harder to remove something that is part of us than it is to let go of something that is only a reaction. So, when I am feeling upset and angry, I try to think, "I have anger." If this emotion is only something I have, I can more easily get rid of it.

But what are we getting rid of? Anger is a big basket into which we put many emotions. We feel anger when we feel fear, when we feel guilt, when we feel that we're helpless, when we feel that we are victims, when we feel separate and alone, when we feel powerless and are seeking something to give back the feeling of power. We feel anger when we feel that we are not good enough. We feel anger when we feel someone has done us wrong. We feel anger when we have done someone else a wrong and we don't want to face the fact. Mostly, we feel anger when we are judging others from our own narrow viewpoint and refusing to broaden our field of vision.

When I drive to the nursing home, I set my cruise control at one mile above the speed limit and keep it there. There are forty-two side-road entrances to that thirty-mile stretch of highway. Deer and elk cross at frequent intervals. A driver has to be alert. Despite the fact that I'm driving above the speed limit, other drivers tailgate me, pass without enough clearance, take dangerous chances with head-on traffic, and put their lives and mine in jeopardy. And of course, I'm subject to road rage, especially on days when I'm facing some tough situation at the nursing home. But my road rage doesn't change the drivers who zip past me. It doesn't slow them down; it doesn't ease whatever demon is driving them; it doesn't make the highway safer. All my road rage has ever done is make me a less safe driver and cause me to arrive at the nursing home exhausted and filled with an emotion that hampers my effectiveness.

Alone in our cars, we all feel separate. It's me *here* and all those other guys out *there*. Isolated by a couple of tons of steel, I begin to forget that those other guys are just like me. They're human, busy, stressed, in a hurry, upset about life, feeling pushed. They're tired, hungry, and far from home. They need to go to the bathroom, make a deadline, make a phone call, keep a date. And I'm just a blue car in their way. They're not thinking about me as a person. They don't care if I arrive at the nursing home angry and upset.

But I *do* care, and I find that if I think about them as real human beings, I am much less likely to get angry. If I can pull over and let them by without too much inconvenience, I do that. I watch out for oncoming traffic and many times have pulled on to the shoulder to allow space for three cars to pass safely or to give the careless passer a place to pull into. I try to release my judgment of their actions and just accept them as human beings who are connected to me by their humanity. I bless them and release them. I find that when I do that, even if I've allowed myself to have anger, it goes away more quickly. The days that I don't even have anger are a triumph, and the drive is much more peaceful, allowing me to be at my best when I reach the nursing home.

Nursing homes are places where anger is easily acquired. Caregiving is a high burnout profession. Wages are generally low. Staff turnover is usually high. The emotional toll of caring for people who are moving toward death is immense. New, untrained staff causes strain in the whole system. Colds and diseases travel quickly through the resident population and the staff, and visitors too, and often the level of health is low. The fatigue level is high. The frustration level is high. Tired, frustrated, powerless, and feeling rotten, we sometimes act as if the only power we can obtain is by taking on a hot, invigorating load of anger.

But does it do any good? For anyone? When someone has unloaded a mess of anger on you, has it ever made you feel really excited and eager about correcting a situation? Stung by someone's anger, have you felt like cooperating, putting forth your ideas for a solution, sitting down for a cohesive conference, joining with others to act as a team?

After you have dumped a load of anger on someone, after the "high" of feeling empowered by a strong emotion, do you really feel good about yourself? Or does the screech of your own anger echo in your mind, making you cringe. And are you suddenly worried that the staff person you yelled at might take out her resentment on your patient? Do you see that staff person's eyes slide away from you when you visit the next time? Do you see her moving out of contact with you, for fear of being burned by more of your anger, stepping back from the cooperation and the friendliness that lubricate close interaction with others?

You cannot survive as a caregiver, nor can you be effective as a caregiver, if you have so much anger that it is in constant danger of erupting. It's hard not to have anger, but there are ways to grow to a point where we don't take on that load of acid.

One way to grow is to broaden our vision of the situation. To do this, we have to remove some of the windowless walls we have put around our own concerns. Inside those walls, we begin to feel that we are the only ones who have ever felt the stress of caregiving, of being rushed, ailing, short on money, and needing more emotional support. If you look away from yourself and open a window on the world, you will begin to feel that you are a part of a vast population that has the same problems. It is much easier not to have anger when you are part of a group called We and not sitting separate from a group called They.

Broadening your vision will not make you wishy-washy or less effective. When you can see the problems of everyone in the situation, you'll be much more likely to see who can solve the problem. One holiday weekend at the nursing home, because of a shortage of staff caused by illness and time off, a young woman was assigned to work alone in the Alzheimer's unit. When I arrived to visit, the anxiety level in the unit was at an all-time high. The patients were tense and restless. The young woman was close to tears. "I've never worked in an Alzheimer's unit before," she said. "I don't know what to do with these people." Feeling totally at sea, she actually sat down and did nothing. My mother was not clean. There were no peaceful activities in progress. The young attendant was paralyzed by fear.

I felt concern, but what good would it have done to blow up? At any rate, the entire institution was so shorthanded that there was no one to protest to. Since the patients knew me better than they knew the attendant, I moved around among them, talking in my usual way, giving a hug here, holding a hand there, and finally going to the piano, as is my usual habit, and playing some of the songs the patients liked. My presence, and my more matter-of-fact way of looking at the patients, helped the young woman for the hour or two I was there. I could not take over her job, but I could ease the situation for that short time, and while there, I could judge for myself if the situation was unsafe for my mother or anyone else. The patients were agitated, but not in danger, so I finally left the unit.

On the following Monday, I went to the director of the institution and asked for a thorough review of the staffing problem of the preceding Friday. Since many people were involved—the director of nursing, the on-duty nurse, the aides themselves—there was no one person who had caused the situation, and, at any rate, I wasn't looking for a place to put blame. I was interested in helping the administrator to be totally aware of the situation so that it would not be repeated. And I wasn't interested in causing trouble for the young woman. I emphasized my belief that she was not the cause of the inadequate staffing of the unit. The managers of the staff should have made different decisions.

The director thanked me for coming directly to him, being matter-of-fact, and not yelling at him, and in days following, I could tell that there had been a widespread discussion followed by some corrective action.

As the guardian of a resident of the nursing home, I've been interviewed several times by inspectors from the state and at length by inspectors from Medicare. I am always honest and detailed in what I say about the nursing home, but I don't use angry or judgmental words, and I always tell the director what I have told the inspectors. I feel that we're all in this together, trying to make a safe, caring environment for our patients.

Another way to keep from having anger is to be honest about what cannot be changed. Any kind of illness has unpleasant factors. In our distress at seeing our own loved patient disintegrating physically or mentally and suffering pain that we cannot ease, we are tempted to indulge in anger at *something*. This anger of frustration etches deep ruts in our own minds and hearts, but it doesn't do one thing to change a condition that is chronic or terminal. Of course it takes mental work to release this type of anger, but the reward for doing so is an easing of the tension in your stomach. And acceptance of what you can't change in one situation transfers to other problems too, helping you to develop a habit of release.

Sometimes when we have anger, we have it because we want someone to be different from who they are. We hate it when anyone points out ways that *we* ought to be different, defending ourselves with a thousand reasons why we do what we do and are what we are. But we often turn around and impose the same demands on others. What a great relief it is to other persons and to ourselves when we stop judging and stop insisting on change.

There is a great difference between a sentence beginning "I want you to …" and one beginning "Would it be possible for you to …?" There is a blessing in simple courtesy, in making a request and not a demand. People respond to courtesy very well, because a request gives them power, while a demand or an order divests them of power. We feel happy and less frustrated when we feel empowered. We also feel happy and less frustrated when we willingly give power. We are giving a gift to another when we imply that we trust their ability to do the most helpful thing that they can do for us. And our trust eases our own fear.

A very hard lesson to learn is one that is most valuable. No one is responsible for my anger but me. Nobody can make me have anger. Nothing that another does can force me to pick up a load of anger unless I find some reward in that anger. It takes real emotional honesty to recognize this, but if you want to look in the mirror and see an easing of those tired hard lines on your face, if you want your gut to stop twisting like the winds in a tornado, if you want to stop having anger, you need to see why you enjoy it. Think of how much fun you've had bitching about someone else's actions. Think of the judging, criticizing, carping, putting down that you've indulged in to make yourself feel better about yourself. Think how much easier it seems to try to blame someone else for our own turmoil. But going around in these circles never stops the turmoil.

I finally learned that if I wanted to survive, I had to change my mind about where I acquired my anger. And I had to learn that I do not want to have anger. Once I learned that I truly do not wish to have anger, it became much easier not to have it, although this lesson is more like a lifelong curriculum than a one-time learning. I believe it is going to be worth the effort. I believe that it is helping me to survive. Caregivers are already carrying an emotional load. The negative emotions of anger are too destructive to be borne.

Chapter Eight

Growing Used to Grief

Grief is a very personal, private emotion. We may get advice from others who have gone through loss and survived, and for a short time after our own losses, we may find someone who will listen as we voice our pain. But loss makes others uncomfortable, and telling someone else about our loss may not be of help. Ultimately, even though all of humanity must suffer loss, as solitary humans, we each endure our grief—as we endure physical pain—alone.

Loss by death gives one a starting point for growing used to grief. From that date forward, the beloved person is not part of the human picture. You are no longer responsible for caregiving, for keeping your vows, for paying attention, for responding, for sharing children, memories, a house, a budget, a car, a life. The one person who could truly understand your loss is no longer there. You must grieve on your own. Even if you take on the job with some knowledge of how others have done it, understanding as best you can your own emotional reactions to loss—even if you are determined to continue to live despite the death of a person and a way of life that seemed so vital that it is difficult to consider living at all—it is still going to take time and energy to move through grief. The first year, you are cushioned by shock and a sense of the nearness of the beloved person; the second year, you begin to realize that this loss is forever; the third year, you come face to face with the barren truth that another's death has changed you, but not released you, and that you must truly make a life that does not include your loved one. And then you move forward alone considering your own options. If you have worked well through your grief, you are stronger and wiser, and you can release the past and be involved in a valuable present life.

The grief of caregivers is different. The dreadful human losses caused by Alzheimer's disease and other debilitating diseases do not give a starting point for grief. Month after month, the patient suffers daily losses of normal abilities. The caregiver must deal with those losses, learning the nursing skills to tend to increasing physical disabilities, finding new ways to communicate with the patient who has lost more mental faculties. The losses pile up in one's mind, but there is never a moment when one can say, "It is done—this person and I have suffered every one of the losses we will handle together, and now I can grieve and go on."

There is not even a stable quality to the losses; they don't progress in a regular manner. Illness is erratic. People rally; people fade, only to rally again. A mental loss that seems permanent for weeks or months with an Alzheimer's patient may suddenly be overcome by some new, unseen, unpredictable occurrence in the patient's brain or psyche.

My mother's ability with words has been a joy for us all, friends as well as relatives. When we were children, she used to play rhyming games at the table. If you wanted to ask someone to pass the peas or the potatoes, you had to put your request into rhyme, which we did with much giggling. Mother's letters were often graced with foolish little verses that would mean nothing to the world, but which were true communication with the person to whom she was writing. She and her own mother often wrote verse to each other. Her father played games with words and humorous stories, many of which she collected with plans to publish. Her vocabulary was extensive. When a family discussion got going, you had to be mentally agile to keep up with Mother's expression of her view of any subject. She had the words, and she knew how to organize them and to release them with passion and power. Her focus in the discussion might irritate you, but you had to admire her skill in debate.

The loss of Mother's word power was not abrupt. Sometimes, in a letter, one word would seem oddly out of place. But we all have such slips of the mind, and it would be overlooked. After she moved to our home, the losses became more severe, more bizarre. One day, while attempting to write a letter, she wrote several perfectly intelligible paragraphs, and then the letter disintegrated. Words were misused. Some words were not completed. Sentences lost sense. That letter became a disaster for her, as great as any shipwreck. She left the table, only to return to look at the letter again and again. Finally, she came to me and pulled me toward the table. "Look at this letter and tell me who wrote it. They mention your father's name, but I can't make out what it means."

I could not help her because she knew only on a subconscious level that she had written the letter herself. She would not let me take the letter away. She would not be distracted by other occupations. All day, she returned to the table in her restless circling of the room, and each time she tried to understand how that strange letter had been written. By nightfall and bedtime, we were both exhausted.

This was a huge loss, but there was no time for grief. The suffering, frightened person was still there, needing more care than ever. That day was only a beginning in the painful, erratic, but ongoing loss of her written and spoken verbal skills. During the last six years, she has gone from making relatively clear, complete conversation to rambling conversation that had meaning only if you possessed clues from knowing her all her life, to conversation that had no meaning at all because the words she used seemed not to be the words she meant, and then to only gestures and short words to indicate what she wanted. During a time when her medication was not right and she was undergoing some dental problems, she stopped speaking almost completely. Recently, though she still speaks less than before, she has regained some clarity, being able to put together an occasional complete sentence that says what she means to say and makes sense.

The caregiver must adjust to each new situation. And there are dozens of situations, not just the loss of words. The body, the mind, the emotions, the spirit—all are connected, and the change is constant. And the caregiver piles up an inner mountain of unexpressed grief.

After my husband became so ill, I had a new buildup of grief. But I was taking care of him, too, and could not give way to the grief. In order to survive, I had to find a way to deal with so many losses.

For me, the undissipated grief caused a terrific lack of emotional energy. I had physical energy and mental energy that allowed me to continue with my duties at home and at the nursing facility, but I began to have difficulty making enough emotional connection with others to carry on a social conversation. I could not even become involved in reading fiction, because I didn't have the emotional energy to care about a fictional character.

I could not cry. There was no place to cry. I would be useless in my mother's care if I cried at the nursing home. My weeping caused stress for my husband, and so it would not release my own emotional tension to cry at home. You can't cry and drive. But more than that, though I could have used the emotional release, it did not seem that it would help to cry. I would just have to dry my eyes and keep on keeping on. I felt those tight lines in my face pull up a little tighter.

And then, with the help of my daughter, who came to stay in our home so that I could go, I went to a convention of Western Writers of America. At that convention were dear people whom I've known for nearly twenty years, but see only once a year. The first thing I learned at the convention was that when you can't cry, you can laugh.

Everybody helped me. Free for five days from the constant duties of caregiving, I allowed myself to *feel* free. Friends gathered around. We had fun, we indulged in foolish conversation. Even our professional conversations were lighthearted. After a few days of laughter, I was able to cry. And when I cried, my friends were tender. I've never been hugged so many times.

I came home with a new vision of what one can do about grief. If my wonderful friends could be so tender with me, I could be more tender with myself. I started caregiving for *me*. Now, I do not go right home after I leave the nursing home. I take half an hour, sometimes an hour, to do some pleasant thing. I like good coffee. A couple of restaurants in our area provide gourmet coffee. I love bookstores. I go to a bookstore and browse. (One bookstore has taken on big-city ways, providing books and gourmet coffee, too.) I take a folder with stationery and sit in Wal Mart's coffee shop and write a letter to a friend. I draw a cup of non-gourmet French vanilla cappuccino from the Wal Mart coffee machine and drive to Sand Lake to sip the sweet hot brew while I watch the ducks and geese or gaze at the winding mists on Mt. Shavano. Sometimes I cry. Sometimes I daydream. Always I stay in my own world, thinking about myself, not thinking of any of the people to whom I give care. I give myself free rein to dream about whatever I choose. No one is listening in. I can be all the past me's, all the potential me's. Freed from the stereotype of responsible, steady, ever-reliable caregiver, I can be a mental gypsy, just like my mother was. Grief will wait until I can attend to it all at once.

Only *you* can know what specific things will help you to find relief, to feel that you have been freed for a few moments from the relentless, grim chores of caregiving. But if you are to survive, you *must* find ways to treat yourself tenderly and well. No one has the right to tell you what will make you feel better. You have *every right* to find out what helps you to feel renewed and refreshed. You are a valuable part of the world. You have the right to say no and to say yes without pressure. You have a right to a few moments of precious privacy. You have a right to tenderness and foolishness and joy. You have a right to ask that the scale be balanced with something that eases the heavy burden of ongoing losses.

We caregivers know that ahead of us we still have to face the death of our patients. If we are totally used up, we may not survive the grieving process that comes with the end of a life. You have the right to survive. Be gentle with yourself.

Chapter Nine

Grow Up and Be Free

In the United States, we are confused about growing up. As children, we weary of the never-ending list of things we should not, must not, cannot do. We look forward to growing up and having the license to do what we choose to do. For most of us, the admonition to *grow up* is often accompanied by some kind of criticism from an authority figure. In a muddled way, we resent the criticism and any well-meant advice as well, as if the adult were trying to take some precious thing away from us. We want to grow up on our own terms in our time for our own reasons.

And then at a certain point in our maturing, being grown up becomes fraught with fear. In our youth-oriented society, we associate the idea of growing *up* with burdens that must be borne until we then grow *old*. We can hardly wait to be sixteen, but we dread turning thirty. We speak of a fiftieth birthday as the BIG 5-0, as if it were more than just another day in a long life. We approach these grown-up birthdays with childish emotions, feeling that something is being taken away from us and something is being expected of us. And our fear delays our true maturity. So we struggle along, still trying to please all the adults.

We may have just reached the point of thinking that we have satisfied our parents and parent-figures by achieving a few of the goals society sees as acceptable, when suddenly the parents become dependent themselves and no longer appreciate our achievements because their needs have changed. The aging parent may now feel that the child's accomplishments are a threat. The ailing parent may feel that the adult child should "come home" and take care of things. And because that child may be the one already designated as "family caregiver," all the old emotional strings pull tight.

To survive as a caregiver, your emotional stability cannot be based upon the expectations of or the rewards from another person. Parents age, spouses fall ill, even grown children have problems. If you're a caring person, needy people will be drawn to you, and you will respond. But your responses need to be rational.

This chapter has been the most difficult of all the chapters in this book to think about and write, because reaching a measure of maturity and peacefulness came so late to me and was so hard to achieve. But the only point in any human pain must come from using that pain to understand another, to extend compassion and sympathy, and to offer others the feeling that they are not alone in a dilemma, and so I share these stories.

The publication of my first novel occurred at a time when my mother was beginning to feel the first frightening losses caused by Alzheimer's disease. We didn't know that she had a disease of dementia, but her reactions to my novel were certainly over-wrought and without sense considering the history of her support for my writing. I wasn't in the position of caregiver for my mother at the time, but her reactions to my book foreshadowed the difficult times ahead. And my private emotional response to her reactions showed me that I was not ready for such difficulties.

I could see *intellectually* that my mother had begun to feel that my writing was a threat to her career and her reputation as a writer. I did not change my professional course, and I even said—quite calmly and rationally and maturely in my opinion—"It would make no sense in my life to stop writing, and it wouldn't really help her."

But it is easy to state that one has become mature. It is not always the truth. One would have thought that, having survived my first husband's death, and gone on to raise a child, to begin a writing career, to re-marry and yet continue writing, that I could have truly faced my mother's response with equanimity. But I could not. When I published my first novel at the age of fifty-two and the fact of that publication upset my mother, I felt like a scolded child, not a grown-up. In the turmoil of her increasing anger and delusions, I did not deal with my emotions.

It was not until several years later, when I *was* her caregiver, that an event caused me at last to see that I *must* grow up completely.

I have always done the research for my novels "in the field," getting hands-on experience. I've been down in mines, out in the night in a lambing shed, and deep in the woods on a bear project. When it came time to write a novel about a woman who ran an airport, I wanted to know enough about flying to be sure that no one reading the book would find anything phony in my depiction of that world. After I interviewed pilots and mechanics and airport staff, I decided that I needed to learn to fly.

Since there was an airport within two minutes driving time of the care unit where my mother was confined, I began to take flying lessons earlier in the mornings of the days I went to see her. I told my mother about the lessons, never certain if she understood what I was doing. Finally, after eight long months of ups and downs, in confidence as well as in the Cessna, I made my first solo flight—three glorious trips around the traffic pattern all alone in the plane, three good landings, and a huge upsurge of wondrous joy.

I went from the solo flight to the nursing home to take my mother for a walk in the May sunshine. Filled with an overwhelming joy of achievement, I told my mother all about the flight, never thinking what an unkind thing I was doing. Her response to the joyous words about my freedom in the air was a confused and confusing attack. Out of the pain of her own bondage, she drew up many critical words. She told me all the ways in which I was failing others. Her words were confused, but the intense emotion caused by her pain gave her the ability to get her meaning across. She was angry and envious and hurt.

Astounded, almost sick at my stomach, I left the nursing home at a terrific low point. But then, I began to reconstruct my joy, determined that nothing could spoil that solo flight. I went to a local gift shop and bought a hand-carved ironwood eagle. I asked the attendant to write a label for the bottom of the piece, naming the date and flight.

Then, taking the eagle with me, I went to a coffee shop, sat with a hot, comforting cup of coffee, and reviewed the visit and my mother's attack. Why had I told her about my solo? At first I tried to convince myself that I had been speaking to her as a friend, thinking that she would be glad for me. Then, I needed to admit that I had also been speaking to her as my mother, hoping that she would add an extra affirmation to my accomplishment.

How immature and how *cruel* I had been. Needing my mother's approval, I had carried my tale to a woman who could no longer be my mother or anyone's mother in the sense we all mean when we demand that type of nurture. And even knowing that she had always yearned to be free in the way that flying set *me* free, I was still so involved in my own need for her praise that it never occurred to me that my news would cause her pain.

Her children had, perhaps, accepted her dementia and her limitations by placing her in the locked unit of a nursing home, but it was obvious that *Mother* was not resigned. Because her words were often so meaningless, it was easy to believe that her thoughts were meaningless. It was painful to know that I had caused her pain. It was more painful to know that beyond the dementia, she was still there with all her needs and yearnings.

Then, at fifty-eight, I *finally* began to grow up. I had to learn how to enjoy being my own self, *for* my own self, without inflicting pain by my attempts to communicate with my mother, my attempts to be affirmed by her. Freed from my need for her recognition and approval, I might be able to look at *her* needs with dispassionate maturity and attempt to meet them in a more rational way. I thought of the many caregivers who had said to me, "My mother no longer knows me." Yes, that is the great fear we all have until we are grown up and free: If my mother doesn't know me, who am I?

And then my husband had a heart attack, and I had some more growing up to do. He was too intensely involved with survival at the time to be concerned about me. For twenty-seven years, he had taken care of me in his own way. I had, for instance, never in that time checked the oil in my own car or had the tires rotated. He always knew about the septic system and the furnace and the water pump. More important, I was used to his hugs and kisses and his warm responses—his affirmation. Busy with his care, I fought new fear—my mother doesn't know me, my husband doesn't love me. But I was still needed by them both. I could hardly walk off to find an affirming world of my own *out there* somewhere.

That restriction in my life proved to be a blessing. Barred from going out in the world to look for a substitute mother, a substitute husband, I was forced to look inside myself for the support and care I needed. *If my mother no longer knows me, then I'd better know myself. If my husband cannot be emotionally supportive right now, then I'd better learn how to go to my inner world for that support.*

Caregivers know that they have responsibilities. Sometimes, caregivers don't know that they also have rights. Feeling bereft, being forced to go inside myself, I began to learn what my needs were and to see that there are many ways of meeting needs when one's situation changes. I continued with my flying and got my pilot's license. Letting some of the housework slide, I went back to writing. After making certain the day was started well for others, I took an hour each morning to read and meditate. I began to know myself and to provide the approval I needed from a larger inner self.

Feeling free to seek my own fulfillment, I began to see that I could allow my mother and my husband their own experiences. I stopped feeling so devastated by the illnesses that were a part of *their* life plans. I learned to ease back a bit from my intense, intrusive focus on my husband's diet-and-medicine-and-weight-and-health regimen. Our society has a habit of telling wives and mothers to *make* their husbands and sons eat the right things, get their exercise, stop smoking, and take their medicine. Commercial after commercial on television makes it seem as if the best wife is the one who is handing over the right toothpaste or the proper vitamin bottle to her clueless male. Well, it is amazing! When I began to grow up, my husband joined me in the process. Little by little, he took over much of his own caregiving, which renewed his confidence in himself and enabled him to renew his care for me.

While my mother cannot take care of herself in many ways, I started noticing that the staff at the nursing home did a better job than I did of helping her to be independent. They were very matter-of-fact. When I was there and Mother was slow to eat, I picked up a spoon and fed her. But after a few hints from the staff, I found that if I waited, she would eventually pick up her spoon and feed herself. Now, even though she no longer feeds herself, I encourage her to co-operate in the eating process, and we work as a team.

I would not write of such private moments of pain and growth if I had not met caregivers who were also in intense pain. It is very, very difficult to take care of others when it seems there is no one to take care of you. But there *is* someone to care for you. It is you. You have a wonderful, capable, giving inner self who guides your wonderful, capable giving outer self. That inner self is made up of all the parts of you. You can find in that self a child to play games with, a friend to talk to, an adult to lean on. Trust that inner self. Suddenly, as you realize that you have *inside* yourself all that you need, you will find that *outside* yourself you also have all that you need. And sometimes, when you yearn for a bit of mothering, you may receive, as I have, such attention from your own child, and you will realize that the mother/daughter/mother/daughter link is ongoing and deeply rewarding, even as the roles change. What a blessing to know that we all grow up, we all grow old, we all *grow!*

Chapter Ten

Reach for Reality

Advice can be maddening when there is no way to follow it. Reports in the news media can be distressing when they offer hope that doesn't apply to you. In order to keep your mind calm and clear as you continue day-by-day with caregiving, it is important to know the truth about your own situation.

We have many myths in our society. One of the most pervasive is that the doctor will always be there, wise and knowing and helpful. There's no point in believing this. It gives one a false hope and puts a terrific burden on doctors. The entire healthcare system is burdened. In a remote area such as ours, there are too few doctors for the population. Some doctors no longer take new patients at all.

When my mother first came to live with us, we could not find a doctor who was willing to accept her as a patient. It would have been convenient to take her to the local medical center, but it was not possible without a local doctor. We finally located a doctor who agreed to oversee her care and to prescribe her medication at a medical clinic thirty-five miles north of our home. He was a giving and understanding doctor with some knowledge of dementia and caregiving, but he was also terrifically busy. After Mother's initial physical exam, the doctor essentially turned her care over to me, consulting with me by phone, making adjustments to the medicine simply by evaluating my reports about her actions and reactions.

When we moved my mother to the nursing home, which is thirty-two miles *south* of our home and out of that doctor's jurisdiction, we had to seek a new doctor. We had to *beg* for a new doctor. Finally, a doctor from a very busy office agreed to oversee Mother's care at the nursing home, but he didn't actually *see* her. He dropped by the nursing home, read other patients' files, read Mother's file, listened to the nurse's reports, and prescribed for her care. I don't know if he saw the other patients, but I do know that he did not recognize my mother on sight. When he moved to a larger city in more populated area, he did not notify us. It was only through a casual remark at the nursing home that I even knew that my mother's doctor had left town.

A fine young doctor took his place. That amazing man actually goes into the locked ward and observes my mother's actions before he orders treatment or prescriptions. But even he is too busy to see her often. He is also too busy to talk to me on the phone. The oft-given advice about talking to one's doctor is not practical to follow when the doctor has gone across a mountain pass to another clinic in a remote town for the day. The doctor and I communicate by letters. I write to him concerning my observations of my mother; he responds with suggestions or he simply orders treatment. To a certain extent, he also depends on my reports, instead of his observation, to help him with her treatment. He is such a caring and responsive physician that I am sure he will have many offers to go to a larger office in a larger city. When he accepts one of those offers, we'll have to begin again to find a doctor to see to Mother's care.

This is reality. I have accepted it. I do not plan to get more than minimal help from the medical community. Our hospital is not staffed to deal well with Alzheimer's patients. I sat with my mother there for three days and nights when she had pneumonia. She was placed in a room where no one could have seen her from the hall, the curtain drawn around the hall-side bed blocking any view of her. When her food was brought to the room, no one told her that it *was* food, and she did not realize that beneath the stainless-steel domes, there were recognizable plates and utensils. Her arthritic hands are not strong enough to lift the stainless-steel covers. The silent curved TV screen mounted near the ceiling across from her bed mirrored a distorted room, which confused her. She kept saying, "That room, that room up there." The actual room was cluttered. It did not seem that the staff had ever read anything about the need of Alzheimer's patients to have clear, almost barren, space because they cannot distinguish necessary objects from others. During the night, my mother tried to climb out of the bed. Had I not been sleeping in the room and waked at the sound, she would have fallen head first with her legs trapped in the side rails of the bed.

In the large hospital where my husband had an angioplasty, he was put afterwards into a cardiac care unit with a sandbag on his incision and told not to move the sandbag, lest he bleed from the artery. Because his lungs were involved, he had to cough often. Because he was groggy from the drugs, he did not realize the meaning of the instructions. Every time he coughed, the sandbag moved from the incision. There was no nurse available. There was no nurse in sight. When a nurse did come in, she once again told a sleeping, coughing, drugged man, "Don't move the sandbag." I sat next to him in a chair, reading a book to stay awake, and at the first rattle in his lungs, I rose and held the sandbag so that it would not move from his groin.

In many ways modern medicine provides miracles. The angioplasty itself seems a miracle. But the caregiver must not take too much for granted. Frustration with medical facilities adds an exhausting burden to the caretaker. The reality of the situation is that the caregiver must often rely on his or her own perceptions and take action. There's no point in fighting reality. Every bit of resentment and anger increases the emotional drain of caregiving. There is wonderful freedom in simply accepting the situation and taking care of your own patient. The need to be alert in the hospital is not a recent development. When my first husband was dying of cancer over forty years ago and vomiting from the prescribed drugs, he was left without any vessel to throw up into while a group of nurses stood in the hall, chatting and ignoring his call light. At that time, I took weeping, angry action. Since I was pregnant at the time, the anger I had did not help me or the situation.

Now I find that it is much easier to speak up calmly for what I want, to insist firmly on getting it, and to be a sharp-eyed overseer until the crisis is over. I am calm and professional in my demeanor, and since I am very clear about my goal—the well-being of *my* patient—others seem to hear the steel in my voice and to respond with appropriate action.

Another myth that we deal with is the one that says, "If you read it, it's got to be true." Despite many public exposes of newspaper articles, we think of the false information as the exception. Medical articles in newspapers are not exactly false, but they are misleading. A reporter can raise your hopes by the way he words an item about a breakthrough in the study of Alzheimer's drugs or the detection of Alzheimer's in the first place. Kind friends will inevitably mail you the article, or you'll read it yourself and get that sudden hope, only to realize that you are reading about a very small study, about drugs which have not been approved and are not available, and that the genetic detection of the disease is not a certainty. The yo-yo effect of medical information in the press can be distressing. What is reported as fact one day is quite often contradicted by other articles in following days. I don't ignore news of possible helpful medications, but I don't take the news seriously when I read it. I believe that medical researchers will eventually discover the cause and the cure for Alzheimer's disease, but my mother is now ninety-seven years old. I don't believe that they will discover the cure for her disease before she dies or in time to reverse the terrible effects it has had on her life, so I don't torture myself with possibilities.

As I said earlier, I have found that the best source of information about drugs is my local pharmacist. The pharmacists in our small town and the one in the town where the nursing home is located are knowledgeable about drugs and drug reactions far beyond any doctor with whom I've ever spoken. Because of the pharmacist, I am aware of what the drugs for dementia are supposed to do. I know that they don't all work in the same way with every patient. I know that the effects of certain medicine weaken after a while. The pharmacist always takes time to talk to me and to explain things clearly. Because of the pharmacist, I was able to find the information that proved that my husband's severe pain and muscle damage, which developed a year after his heart attack, were actually being *caused* by the medicine prescribed to help his heart. The pharmacist knows which medicines interact to cause harmful side effects. I have never met an indifferent pharmacist. Perhaps I'm lucky, but it adds a great deal to my peace of mind to have found a dependable source of information.

It is easier to survive when you recognize what is real and what works for you. Every situation is different. Even the pamphlets from professional organizations do not speak to you as an individual. You'll know that you've found your own reality when you feel calm and peaceful about the actions you take. Being certain, you will feel more joy in what you do. My husband and my mother are not "subjects of a study," and my caregiving actions are not theories. By seeing the reality of my patients' conditions, by accepting the reality of the available help, and by understanding the reality of my own limitations, I found a solid, successful course of action. But I urge you: Don't seek my reality, don't feel that you *should* do anything I suggest. Find your own reality. It's the only one that will work for you.

Chapter Eleven

Mind the Moment

By this point in this book, you may be strongly irritated by me and all my words. "How can I possibly be calm," you may ask me, "when I have so much to do, so many demands, so little time, so little money?" I know what you mean. I've read dozens of self-help books and argued mentally with the authors. How can one possibly accomplish all that must be done?

One *cannot* accomplish all that must be done. One can only do what must be done in this moment. Learning to focus on the present moment is probably one of the hardest tasks I've ever taken on. Being responsible for the family bill paying, housecleaning, laundry, correspondence, medical checking, pill pushing, cooking, counting of fat grams and food exchanges, pet care, letters to doctors, calls to and from the nursing home, contact with family and friends, calls to my agent, editing for clients, sending out books and manuscripts, answering fan mail, maintaining a professional wardrobe, reading professional literature, attending book signings, teaching seminars, and all the rest of it, I always thought that I *had* to be thinking on several levels at the same time. I was convinced that if I wasn't busy mentally organizing the next task while doing the present task, I would never get everything done.

The truth is that by splitting my focus, I was not getting more done. I was doing many things in a haphazard, incomplete way. Soon, I began to forget even the little that I had done—where I had put my keys or the new prescription or the letter from the doctor. I wasted time trying to recapture my memory of where I had left tools, unpaid bills, new credit cards. I couldn't remember if I had answered a letter. The pantry shelf was incompletely stocked, even as I finished grocery shopping. It finally got to a point where I would go to the pantry or to the bedroom and stand there wondering what I sought. Or I would drive to town to mail a letter, but leave that letter on the kitchen counter.

I simply had to change, to learn a better way of using my mind.

But my mind was a mess, so I started with my environment. Categories are very comforting. I set up my file cases, my desk, and my life with categories. In the household file, there is a folder labeled "Bills to Pay," one for "Receipts to Post and File," and several folders where I put those receipts necessary when I compile information to file my income tax return. In the box where we kept my husband's medicine, there was a file card showing the current dosage for each medication. Near my household desk is a cabinet with drawers. In the top drawer are "Letters to Answer" In the middle drawer, I have stationery and envelopes at hand—and all those nice blank note cards we get in the mail. At the bottom are "Letters to Save."

When Arthur was alive, we turned "mail time" into a pleasant occasion on which I sat down with him, and we shared what had been delivered to our box. Now, I continue to deal with the mail completely every day. I throw away the junk mail (except for those note cards) and I make one circuit of the house, filing the rest in the appropriate folders.

I have categories for the days in my life, as well. Certain days I pay bills, certain days I visit the nursing home, certain days I write letters, certain days I go downstairs to my professional office and work on a manuscript. If I'm going to the nursing home, I take a list of whatever shopping is necessary and do it on the way back. If I'm staying home, I put all the machines in the house to work for me so that I can get a lot done in the particular place where I am. I don't go away from home for errands on my stay-at-home days.

Today is a stay-at-home day. Before coming to this office to write, I put a load of clothes in the washer and one in the dryer. (During Arthur's life, I would have made his lunch and left it available.) The dishwasher will take care of at least hiding the dishes until I can get back to the kitchen.

The answering machine will pick up the phone. While I am downstairs in my writing office, I am thinking only of this chapter. If something occurs upstairs to which I *must* attend, I turn my focus to the interruption, but once the crisis is over, I return my focus to the computer screen.

It takes long and constant practice to learn to focus only on what you are doing at any given moment. But the results are wonderful. You get much more done. You are not nearly so tired. That frazzled, irritated, frustrated feeling dissipates. It is refreshing to be so well focused that time stops and you are not aware of its passing.

There are additional benefits to focusing on the moment. When I am at the nursing home, I think only of my mother and her environment. I take time to note her condition. Is she more or less alert? Does she have new bruises? Does she seem restless or anxious? Is she eating well? Is there new staff in the unit? Is the area clean and odor free? Are her clothes well coordinated? (When her blouse is bright red and her slacks are pink, I go find a staff person and ask for a change of clothes. Mother notices how she looks, and she doesn't like clashing colors.) By the time I've visited with the staff, walked with my mother and other patients in the unit, shared the day's lunch, and "felt" the emotional atmosphere of the unit, I have enough information about the situation to be able to relax, to leave the nursing home and focus my mind elsewhere. As soon as I am out the door, I take a deep breath, look at the sky and the mountains, and turn my mind toward the grocery list or my visit to the bookstore. I release thoughts of the actions I've taken to change things in my mother's situation and draw my mind away from those things which cannot be changed.

Before Arthur's death, I used music in the car to keep my mind peaceful so that when I arrived home I was ready to focus on him and his report of his afternoon. When my attention was fully on him, I noticed the small signs that told me that I needed to check his glucose or adjust the evening meal. And it seemed that when I gave him my complete attention, he returned more attention to me. Our focus on each other improved our sense of companionship. If I had not seemed distracted and I had really listened to him, he was cheerful about releasing me to my next task or to a few moments of relaxation.

If I go for a walk for recreation, I don't spend the time thinking of what I will do when I get back. I enjoy my surroundings and sometimes don't think at all. It is not possible to do a chore while walking in the woods, so why drag that chore into my mind and spoil the walk?

Sometimes I wake up in the night with tasks whirling around in my head, and most often the subject is the budget. It makes absolutely no sense to try to balance income and outgo at three o'clock in the morning, but controlling my mind at that time has been one of the hardest things to learn. Focusing on sleep does not make one sleep. So I've learned to pick up a book or to meditate. My meditation is more or less mental chatter at first, but if I persist, I can release the bills and the budget and move into a quiet mental place which often leads me right into sleep. (Gurus may say that if you fall asleep when you're meditating, you're not doing it right, but gurus aren't in my head at three o'clock in the morning, and I'm delighted with the outcome of my change of focus.)

Focusing is not an easy thing to learn or to practice in a life filled with myriad detailed duties. But when you have finally mastered the moment, you will find that the change in your mind leads you to a much calmer, more peaceful interior place. You will have taken one more important step toward surviving as a caregiver.

Chapter Twelve

Change with Change

Despair can be devastating. And the inevitable downward spiral of Alzheimer's disease, or any other terminal disease, can cause despair for the caregiver. Most of the suggestions in the preceding chapters can be a help—accept your choice, know the disease, give up guilt, mind the moment—but the fatigue caused by the sense of helplessness to stop a downward progression may be nearly overwhelming. The losses are so sad that one dams up grief and tears.

When my mother entered the nursing home, she was still able to read, to make fairly intelligible conversation, to understand conversation and written notes. She made many clever jokes and even continued punning. She could feed herself and chew her food. Once she had been reassured that I would not let her get lost, she enjoyed walking with me and would stroll a mile or more, looking at the scenery and making comments on houses in the neighborhood. I frequently took her out to lunch at different restaurants in town. She liked to go shopping at a grocery store and push the cart.

Gradually, she lost certain abilities. She no longer enjoyed reading or listening to poetry, even her own. The notes I wrote, which at first would engross her for an hour or more, became a painful exercise to her and to me when she could no longer find meaning in the words. I stopped taking her to most restaurants, because if I wasn't watching, she made messes that were unpleasant for the staff and other customers. One day in a small cafe, for no apparent reason and without warning, she picked up her coffee cup and poured all the coffee into the sugar bowl. For quite a while, I could take her to Kentucky Fried Chicken and get a fairly healthy meal by going through the buffet line. Since *everybody* makes a mess at KFC, it wasn't unpleasant, and the staff was very welcoming. But after she had surgery on a growth in her mouth, she could no longer chew the chicken she loved so much. We switched to softer foods in the buffet. But then, the disease took another turn and her brain would not allow her to sit still long enough to eat a meal. In a public place, I could not keep her from getting up and annoying others. Sometimes I could not even keep her from leaving the facility.

Riding in the car still seemed to give her pleasure, but many times when we returned from the drive she refused to get out of the car. Neither I nor the staff could change her mind, and so what had been a pleasure ended up an ordeal. There is no way to appeal to reason when the brain refuses to send appropriate messages.

As the verbal loss increased, Mother and I no longer carried on even limited conversations. Now, she makes an initial attempt to communicate when I first arrive at the nursing home, but her welcome is more often just the recognition in her eyes, and some days even that recognition is missing.

A caregiver comes to a point of not wanting to go at all, of wanting to run away. But the truth of caregiving is that even if you take a day off, the need is still there, and you will go back to certain continued deterioration. Just walking into the nursing home becomes an effort, because you don't know what you will find in the locked unit. The nursing home itself becomes one big symbol of loss and death and despair.

At this point in your caregiving, it is important to find a new perspective. One way to do this is to individualize everyone in the facility. People often speak of the nursing home by saying such things as "all those old people are depressing." Any time we clump precious, unique individuals under a term that de-faces them, we will be depressed. But we can be cheered by seeing the residents in a new light.

Each individual accepts the aging process in a different way. Some people rage at it. And what joy you can find in that rage! Here is an indomitable, stubborn, persevering human being who will not be downed, who has anger and uses it as one powerful outlet for all the frustrations. My own father was one of those. Once, in the hospital, when he was upset by the treatment he had received and I tried to calm him down, he threw his breakfast at me, dish by cup by glass. As I dodged the utensils and saw the orange juice run down the wall, I was amazed at the energy in that eighty-eight-year-old man. I could see what had helped him to survive childhood years of hard labor, the anguish of the Depression, the loss of health and eyesight and hope. What a refreshing storm he created. The room was filled with determination, resolve, and ferocious energy.

Many men in the nursing home voice that same rage. I can hear them cursing everything in sight. Even some women allow themselves to scream obscenities. The honesty of old people is like the honesty of children. Everything phony and artificial has been removed, and the cleansing quality of their open emotion is like a good hot shower. Since my having anger in the nursing home would *not* have a cleansing effect on my relationship with the staff, I partake of vicarious relief of emotion through the residents' responses.

Quiet observation of the sympathetic and caring staff has shown me that the residents are not expressing anger at their care. They are expressing all their yearnings for a life gone by, a home that no longer exists, relationships with people no longer living. As I join with them in the experiencing of these universal emotions, my own depression is lessened by the sharing.

Now, as I pass through the outer areas of the nursing home, I take time to appreciate the individuals who are not my patients. It has become a game with me to coax a smile from one very angry man. There is a delicious spark in his eye when he finally gives in to humor, and he and I both enjoy the moment. A sense of humor is a great weapon for fighting despair.

A woman who sits in her wheelchair with a scowl on her face most of the time sometimes sings songs to herself. One day I discovered that we both sing in the key of G. Now, if she is frowning or weeping, I stop for a moment and begin the words to "Red River Valley." She will immediately pick up on them and sing the song with me. When we finish, she always smiles and says, "Thank you, honey."

Even people who do not respond are interesting. When an aged tree falls in the woods, we do not think of it as ugly or useless. Because of scientific studies, we know that the tree disintegrates slowly and at each point nourishes part of the natural world around it. Our society has a mindset against human aging, but that doesn't mean that the caregiver needs to adopt that bias. The process of human aging may be as nourishing as the tree's return to the earth. We simply have to learn more about the blessings it affords. As an old person seems to lose faculties, perhaps he is only transferring them elsewhere, replenishing a larger spiritual world than we can embrace at the moment.

Changing my view of the nursing home and its inhabitants makes my entry into the facility less stressful. The whole world there is as busy and interesting as an anthill. The staff members are individuals too. Each has a story. Sometimes a staff member tells me her story; sometimes I just observe some little drama that is being enacted among a group of staff members or among staff and patients. Despite the nature of the facility, it is absolutely filled with *life*.

I've discovered, to my amusement, that I am part of the drama for some people. I always wear a hat. People in the nursing home are very much aware of hats. The activities director often schedules a "hat day." I hear comments nearly every visit about my hats. They amuse some people, delight others, perhaps annoy the occasional individual, but invariably my hats bring reactions from staff and patients. Those comments have made me more careful of how I dress to go to the nursing home.

Once when my mother was still articulate, she said, "My guests always look nice." Since my clothes bring pleasure to her and to the other residents, who often reach to touch a necklace or feel a colorful sweater, I try to dress to please them. In the Alzheimer's unit especially, the residents are no longer allowed pins and rings or anything that might be a hazard to them, so I wear my jewelry for their pleasure. One lady tells me how she used to shop in Manhattan, and her lighted eyes linger on my necklace or earrings. Once when I wore topaz beads and sat by my mother's bed, she raised a finger to them and said, "Like falling leaves." Despite her loss of words, when she does speak, she's still a poet.

Even in the Alzheimer's unit, where one might assume that the patients, because of their particular type of loss, would be less unique as individuals, one can be refreshed and surprised. Pay attention to gestures and body language and facial expression, and you can communicate fairly well with people whose verbal ability is lost. It is amazing how much humor the patients in an Alzheimer's ward can share with you if you're tuned in to them. They are able to enjoy their lives on their own level, and if you're willing to slow down and join them, you can share their joy.

It is this paying attention to the individual that eases despair. My mother is not alone in her situation. She is part of an entire world made up of individuals with their own personalities. She is aware that she has a new family in the unit. One day, when we returned from a ride and entered the locked unit, two of the residents stood hand in hand just inside the door. Mother, who had not said a word during the entire ride, said, "I know *these*." She took an offered hand, and the three of them wandered off down the hall like sisters or playmates. There are some residents with whom she clashes, especially when she tries to dominate them, grabbing a hand and pulling the person somewhere she doesn't wish to go. But those situations provide drama, and Mother has a world—she has a viable life—there in that unit, where she is recognized by other residents and cared about by the staff. If I suspend judgment and look clearly at the situation, I might honestly say that she is happier, in this new home with these new friends, than she was in her lonely house without my father, frightened by imaginary sounds from the crawl space and terrified by her own losses.

The burden of *my* idea of what constituted an acceptable life for my mother was wearing me down, eroding my energy, destroying my peace of mind. I had to learn that life itself is the antidote to despair. I needed to give up my judgment of what life is or should be. I had simply to accept life as it happens, where it happens, in whatever changing form.

Chapter Thirteen

Give to Get

The title of this chapter sounds entirely selfish and cold-hearted, but the rewards of some types of giving far outweigh the gift, benefitting everybody. And if you think I contradict myself by asking you to give more, be patient with me, I still have your interests in mind.

One cannot be in any environment on a regular basis over a period of time without becoming familiar with the particular needs of the residents, without seeing times when those needs are not being met. It is difficult to provide activities for Alzheimer's patients, because such patients require intense one-on-one attention, and few facilities can afford to supply enough staff to give such attention. It is also difficult, because of the character of the disease, to find volunteers who are willing to work in an Alzheimer's unit.

The attention of the Alzheimer's patient is not just limited, it is erratic. An activity which engrosses a patient on one day might hold no interest at all the next. When a volunteer prepares an art project or any other project, she can prepare her part of it thoroughly and well, but that might not guarantee the success of the endeavor, as it would in a more normal environment. Because the residents are highly susceptible to any change, the mere presence of the volunteer may cause them anxiety. Any nervousness on the part of the volunteer might cause the patients to feel nervous themselves. An earlier upset of their routine, a change of staffing personnel for the day, even a change in the barometer, and the residents may lose their ability to take part in an activity with any degree of focus.

Alzheimer's patients cannot even take part as spectators in the way that a volunteer might expect. The type of damage that the disease causes in a person's brain may make that person so restless that he or she cannot sit still or stay in one place. It is disconcerting to a person who is giving any sort of presentation to have members of the audience suddenly stand and leave the room. In the regular world, the volunteer might rightly assume that something in the presentation had offended the persons who got up and left. But the volunteer cannot be hurt by the actions of the Alzheimer's patient.

It is important to look for the positive reactions and to ignore the negative reactions. It is vital not to have negative reactions oneself. The patients are very susceptible to negative emotion. To build rapport with them, one must accept the entire situation to such a complete point that one is relaxed and calm no matter what goes on in the unit.

One way to control one's own negative reactions is to change them to neutral reactions. Stop judging the actions of the people in the unit—staff and patients alike—and much of the tension goes out of your response. Take the time to observe the unit and learn its regular routines. If you walk into the unit one day and there is an unpleasant odor, you will not be so upset if you have observed that the staff usually deals quickly with bathroom emergencies. The odor is probably so recent that housekeeping has not had a chance to respond. (If there are *always* odors, and you have any doubts about the cleanliness of the unit, you should be talking with the director, or your patient should not be in that nursing home at all.)

If you have decided to volunteer in some way in the unit, you need to know the staff and the patients as well as the routines. You will have learned a lot about the unit already, simply by visiting your own patient. You can learn more by sitting quietly and watching the interaction of staff and staff, patients and staff, and patients and patients.

When you volunteer, choose an activity that gives you pleasure. If you are relaxed and confident about your own skill, then you can direct your attention to ways of providing the activity to the patients so that they can enjoy it to the best of their abilities.

Choose an activity that does not require a lot of staff work or much of staff time in providing materials for the residents' use. Nursing homes have difficulty keeping enough staff because the jobs are high burnout and low paying. An overburdened staff will not welcome extra duties imposed by a volunteer, even if the volunteer is providing an activity for the residents. If your activity is going to make a mess, plan to clean it up on your own.

You may be saying in your mind right now, "Why on earth is she suggesting that I volunteer at all? I'm already overloaded as a caregiver."

I suggest that you volunteer because it may be a way to ease your own emotional stress when your particular patient begins to go downhill at a faster rate, and you are overwhelmed with the sadness which that decline brings to you.

Though my mother's world had closed in on her, and she and I could no longer share a luncheon date at a restaurant, and even though she had lost the ability to have a conversation, she was still aware of how much time I spent in the unit and was unhappy if I left before she could release me emotionally. I could not bear the memory of her standing at the window of the locked door, looking after me with a strained, unhappy gaze. I needed to stay until her emotional needs for that day's visit were met.

Over the course of the years in which she has been in the unit, my mother has become aware of the pattern of my visits. One day when I prepared to leave, she kissed me and released me and said, "Keep the rhythm." Once when I returned from a ten-day visit to my daughter's home in Mexico City (to help with her newborn child), my mother was furious with the small gift I brought her. She had suffered from the lack of my visits and was not mollified by the gift. It was apparent then, that for her emotional well-being, she needed a routine she could count on.

But if we could not talk as before, I could not find a way of spending the time with her that would allow me to stay comfortably in the unit. It made me so nervous just to be there and do nothing that it made *her* nervous. I tried reading to her and playing games with her and even just walking up and down the halls with her, but the visits were not satisfying to her, and they were exhausting to me.

One day, a staff member asked me if I thought their piano was in tune. I only play by ear, but to oblige her, I sat down and played a song or two. A small woman resident with a walker came immediately to the piano with a light in her eyes that I had not seen before. Because she was so eager for the music, I played another song or two. My mother was rambling up and down the hall, but as I played, she came in and approached the piano bench. She smiled at me and patted my shoulder. Then she wandered out again. She knew I was there, and she was happy with what I was doing.

When I returned for the following visit, a staff member told me that the small woman had talked about the piano music every day that I was gone. Playing the piano seemed to be a way that I could stay in the unit comfortably while reassuring my mother and giving pleasure to at least one resident.

Since that time, my role as the "music lady" has expanded considerably. There is something about music that reaches a different part of the brain than that which is damaged by the disease. Other residents began to join us in the salon when I played. Knowing approximately what years they had been in their teens and early twenties, I tried to play songs that they would have known then. (It seems that the songs we heard when we were falling in love are the songs that bring us pleasure all our lives.)

I'm not a trained pianist. If, for one moment, I stop listening to the song in my head, I make mistakes. I had to learn how to concentrate on the music without losing my focus on the residents, but it was fun, because it is the type of music making I've always enjoyed. My husband and I used to invite our neighbors in to make music together, and it was that pleasant memory that brought me to asking the staff if they had any rhythm instruments that the residents could use. They provided a motley collection in a plastic box.

My small smiling friend took immediately to the bells. Another resident likes to use a wooden hammer on a drum made of a tin can with a plastic lid. A rattle satisfies another patient, and one woman in a wheelchair likes to have the tambourine on her tray, where she can bang on it in time to the music. A delightful man with a great sense of rhythm took the sticks one day and played the other tambourine as a drum.

What glorious racket we make! After each song, we applaud each other and laugh. Forty-five minutes or an hour goes swiftly by. One day I said to my mother, "I have to go and play for the family." Though she is not one of the ones who joins in, she beamed with pleasure, and her eyes sparkled. At first when I made music, she would wander by to pat my shoulder and smile and then wander away again. Once she even said, "Nice music." I think that she is proud that, through me, she is contributing something to the "family." Now that she is less mobile, she sits on a couch in the music room and moves her hands and feet in time to the music.

At Christmas, because the staff wanted the residents to sing carols, I brought my baritone uke to the unit and sang. I have occasionally sung from a stage, even once in a while with a spotlight on my face, and I have not enjoyed that. But when I sit in a circle in the Alzheimer's unit and sing hymns and carols and all the old songs I know, including the country-and-western songs that cause some of my residents to tap their feet, I am filled with joy. Every face in the circle smiles at me. People dance their feet about and play their rhythm instruments. We are having fun. Fun is a wonderful reward no matter where one finds it, but fun in an Alzheimer's ward is a gift for everyone involved. The staff smiles, the patients smile, my mother beams, and I am relaxed and happy.

I now play the piano or sing each time that I visit the unit. That special magic that happens whenever people make music together has happened to us. When I play "Show Me the Way to Go Home" and then rise from the piano to say goodbye, several pairs of arms are outstretched to me. The women want to hug and kiss me. Many of them say, "I love you." One elderly woman says, "I love you, kid," to me—a seventy-two-year-old, white-haired woman. The man who likes "Your Cheatin' Heart" sends silver sparkles from his eyes. The man who is so good at rhythm gives me a big smile and pats my shoulder and tells me to come back. My mother smiles and accepts my kiss and hug of goodbye. I have stayed in the unit long enough for her to feel emotionally satisfied without my being emotionally exhausted.

The quality of my music is not what matters to my friends in the nursing home. It is the *sharing* of the music that brings the smiles to their faces and the light to their eyes.

Any skill that is your own, whether you're professional or amateur, will bring you more joy when you share it with your patient and her "family." Don't feel obligated to do what does not feel natural and joyful. Don't allow the staff to dictate to you what you should do or when or how you should do it. (Remember, you don't need those exhausting *shoulds.*) But if you have an ability that brings you pleasure, you can share it to make the long, long road of caregiving seem less arduous. What I give is a rather loud, flawed piano recital of old out-of-date tunes. What I get is laughter, love, kisses and hugs, and the beautiful light that comes into a room when many individuals are suddenly united and feel as one.

Chapter Fourteen

Look to the Light

A friend of mine had eighteen strokes in nineteen months. Each attack on his brain caused a different sort of reaction. During one of the crises, he went into a coma. To the physicians, nurses, and his family, he was totally unresponsive, never opening his eyes or speaking or moving. After some days, he came out of the coma. He told his wife, "While I was apparently gone from you, I was actually completely there as myself. I tried to open my eyes, to move, to speak. I tried to tell you 'Don't leave. I can hear you. Stay with me.'" In the months before his death, he wrote letters to me with the help of his nurse. The letters arrived in large packets, the words scrawled in huge erratic letters, sometimes just one word to a page. The content of his letters was the same as the content of our former conversations. His depth of self had not changed because the form of his communication had altered.

Scientific studies have shown that we each have unique fingerprints, a unique voiceprint, and DNA that identifies us in the tiniest part. I have come to believe that we each have as well a unique "self print." I believe that even when the outer, material self changes, the inner self is not altered. I cannot prove this scientifically, because we know of no study that identifies a unique "self." But during the years in which I have worked with patients of one sort or another, no matter what their illness and no matter if it was terminal, as the condition of the body deteriorated, there was something that remained whole.

That whole self seems to be made of a lovely form of light. This is, of course, not a new idea. Many, many people have spoken of auras and great rays and other forms of light around bodies. But our society does not know how, as yet, to study the light that so many have seen, and I would not venture to tell a scientist that I have proof of such a light that he can test. I speak only of my own experience and the joy that it has brought me.

Three times, as humans I loved were nearing death, I saw a light around them, a golden glow that gave them a brighter appearance. Each time I saw that light, I felt an expansion of the world, even when I didn't understand what was happening. The light was comforting and loving, and it belonged to the person around whom it glowed. I began to think of light as the essence of what we are.

Then I began to notice that when we as humans are moved deeply by something, we react with sparks of light. My granddaughter's eyes give off sparks when she has an intense emotion. And when she laughs, those sparkles of light fly all about. Often, when two people catch the gist of a joke at the same moment, their eyes meet and they share a kind of light. Lovers have a light in their eyes when they gaze at each other. When that light occurs, it gives us a thrill. We feel more intensely alive for that moment, as if we have been re-energized. (Creatures other than human seem to have this essence of light, too. I have noticed that my dog's eyes show a quick spark of light when I say, "Do you want to go for a walk?")

Of course, I know that there are those who will scoff at what I say, but if you look for the light, you will see small gleams of it almost everywhere. And when you find yourself in a situation where all the negative emotions have taken over—where there is anger or fear or hatred—you will be aware of how dark the situation seems to be. We speak of being in a dark mood, a black mood. We have the blues. We're gloomy. Each of these statements proclaims a lack of light.

This lack of light seems particularly apparent in such hopeless diseases as Alzheimer's and other incurable ailments. But I have discovered, during the years I've accompanied my mother on her journey, that the Alzheimer's unit and the patients in that unit are filled with light. Despite a disease that robs them of communication, behind the physical symptoms, these people are *whole*. (And when Arthur's body was almost dead of cancer, Arthur himself glowed with a light that I can neither describe nor explain.)

During our trips out among strangers when my mother drew strongly on her energy, and her face lit up and she reached out, I began to learn that she was still there—with all those characteristics that had made her the person we knew. The staff mentions the light in Mother's face each time she sees a child. We use the term "her face lit up" very casually, but there is truth in that often-used statement. Somewhere, behind all the damaged equipment in my mother's brain, behind all the outward losses, there is the whole person who is totally aware. When that awareness comes through, it comes as a flash of light in my mother's eyes. When I see that light, whether it comes in response to a joke, to her recognition of me, or to the sight of her grandchildren, it gives me renewed energy to continue to provide real care, care of the whole person.

One day, in an attempt to let my mother know that I was aware of her essence and the self of light, I sat down beside her bed and made sure that she was looking at me so that she could read my lips, even if she couldn't hear me. I said, "I want you to know that I know that you ... the same old Evelyn ... are there inside you despite the fact that you cannot express yourself in the old ways of communicating. I promise you that I will always look to that person and reach to that person."

I had no idea when I began my comments what the results would be. But as I spoke and she concentrated on my lips, a light began to glow in her eyes. When I finished, she struggled to find words. Her mouth twisted and she took a deep breath, and then she said, "Sounds good."

Thrilled by what I considered an affirmation, I began to look with new eyes at all the patients, and I found that light spills out all over the place. Tall Barry sparks like a lit match when he recognizes a tune. The light he gives off is silver, and it lingers in the corners of his eyes. In Jane's brown eyes, the light that comes—when I finally make an appropriate response to her attempts to tell me something—is a rich tawny gold color, and it seems to dwell in the center of her eyes at the top of the iris. The lights in May's eyes, as she listens to music, dance in constant motion like gleaming water in a fast running creek. When the whole rhythm band laughs and applauds itself, light sparkles among us.

In his hospital bed in our living room, when he was too ill too speak, Arthur's eyes would light up with humor or affection. That light rested my tiredness and eased my loneliness.

Each time I see the light, I find that it heals and rests me for that moment. At those times, I am convinced that the disease, whatever it is, is not the patient's *condition*. It is an experience the patient is having, perhaps even to bodily death. But the patient's true condition is elsewhere in the light.

And by looking at my role as caregiver in a new light, I find it easier and easier to change my mind. I am less tired and more certain of how to live this experience. I have less anger, more peace, and more joy.

I should like to repeat what I said in the introduction of this book: To find peace in the midst of turmoil, it is necessary to recognize that it is our own emotions that roil the waters. I have offered examples of some of the changes in my own emotions that have brought me back from emotional exhaustion, but these are not changes that I say the caregiver *should* make. Caregivers do not need *shoulds*. If my words make sense to you, if they bring you hope and point a way toward equilibrium, if they offer comfort, then accept them with my love and respect.

You yourself are filled with light. Look to the light.

Additional Resources

I have included here only books that I have read and that I feel show true understanding of the caregiver. Each of these books lists other sources. Every book written to help a caregiver is important because people differ in their ability to accept help. What touches one reader will not reach another. The need for caregivers is growing at a fast pace. As people in a civilized society, we must acknowledge and cherish those who choose to become caregivers.

Books:

Berman, Claire, *Caring for Yourself While Caring for Your Aging Parents, How to Help, How to Survive,* G. K. Hall and Co., Thorndike, Maine, 1996

Carter, Rosalynn, with Susan K. Golant, *Helping Yourself Help Others,* Times Books, Random House, New York, 1994

Greenberg, Vivian E., *Respecting Your Limits When Caring for Aging Parents.* Jossey-Bass Publishers, San Francisco, 1989

Kouri, Mary K., Ph.D., *Keys to Survival for Caregivers,* Barron's, New York, 1992

Luterman, David, D. Ed., *In the Shadows: Living and Coping with A Loved One's Chronic Illness.* Jade Press, Bedford, MA 01730, 1995

Mace, Nancy L. and Rabins, Peter V. *The 36-Hour Day: A Family Guide to Caring for People with Alzheimer's, Other Dementias, and Memory Loss in Later Life* (4ᵗʰ Edition) A Johns Hopkins Press Health Book, paperback, October 9, 2006

Smith, Douglas C., *Caregiving: Hospice-Proven Techniques for Healing Body and Soul,* Macmillan, New York, 1997

Websites:

http://www.nfcacares.org
The National Family Caregivers Association

www.eldercare.gov
U. S. Administration on Aging's Eldercare Locator

http://www.caregiver.com
Today's Caregiver magazine

ELAINE LONG'S NEW NOVEL IS QUITE A SURPRISE!

Lone Wolf Suite...a Musical, Biographical Novel is a story told in song and presented on a CD. It was produced at the Western Jubilee Warehouse in Colorado Springs, CO. Words and music are by Elaine Long. She also sings the lead with Teclia Cunningham on violin, Brian Pence on drums, and Butch Hause on guitar. The CD was released April 4, 2008.

Notes from the back cover of the CD: "Lone Wolf Suite asks much of the listener. Each song tells part of the story. Each song is connected to the next. The keys and tempos change—sometimes in mid-song—to enhance the mood and timing of the plot. Musical themes appear and disappear, then return with different lyrics that carry the story to its climax."

1. "The Posse Took the Pony"

2. "Lone Wolf on the Ridge"

3. "Let That Cowboy Go"

4. "The Minstrel's Song"

5. "Something More"

Lone Wolf Suite may be ordered through The Book Haven, 128 F. Street, Salida, Colorado 81201
tel. 719-539-9629 or online at Haven@thebookhavenonline.com

New copies of Elaine Long's novels: Jenny's Mountain, Bittersweet Country, and Bear Ridge may also be ordered through The Book Haven.

CPSIA information can be obtained at www.ICGtesting.com
Printed in the USA
LVOW11s0053130716

496079LV00001B/79/P